Donald McCormick, who writes under the name of Richard Deacon, was born in 1911 at Rhyl. He started writing at an early age and subsequently became a journalist. He served in the Royal Navy in the Second World War; his duties included some field work for Ian Fleming in Naval Intelligence. After the war he was editor of the *Gibraltar Chronicle* before joining Kemsley Newspapers where he became Commonwealth Correspondent. He later worked at the *Sunday Times* as Foreign Manager from 1963 to 1973.

Under both his pseudonym and his real name he has written over fifty books ranging from biographies to a novel, but he has principally made a name for himself as a specialist on espionage and the world of intelligence, with histories of the British, Russian, Chinese, Israeli and Japanese secret services. His autobiography *With My Little Eye: Memoirs of a Spy-Hunter* was published in 1982, *'C'*, a biography of Sir Maurice Oldfield, head of MI6, appeared in 1985, *The Truth Twisters*, on disinformation, in 1987 and *Spyclopaedia,* a handbook of espionage, in 1988.

He is married and lives in Beckenham, Kent.

SUPER SPY

The man who infiltrated the Kremlin and the Gestapo

RICHARD DEACON

Futura

A *Futura* Book

ISBN 0 7088 4528 2

Printed and bound in Great Britain by
The Guernsey Press Co. Ltd, Guernsey, Channel Islands

Futura Publications
A Division of
Macdonald & Co (Publishers) Ltd
66-73 Shoe Lane
London EC4P 4AB

A member of Maxwell Pergamon Publishing Corporation plc

CONTENTS

1

ONE NIGHT IN NEW YORK

It was sometime in August 1942 that I met the man whom I shall always remember as the Super-Spy everyone missed. Few have ever heard of him and yet his record is such that he must rank among the ablest and most daring spies of modern times. I only met him once, and at that time I never thought he was a spy. Many times since I have mentally kicked myself for not having asked him more questions. Not that I should necessarily have been given the answers I wanted.

It was many years later that I recalled this meeting and the name he used at the time. There were a few missing pieces in one of those espionage jigsaw puzzles which a researcher gets entangled in from time to time, and I suddenly had a strange feeling that the answer was somewhere or other deep in the recesses of my memory, or, if not the whole answer, at least part of it.

It was not easy to recall specifically any one of those nights I spent in New York in the late summer of 1942. I was waiting for a ship which was still being built at Philadephia, a long way distant, and life ashore was one long series of parties. Something else which militated against efficient recall was the fact that the keeping of a diary was not allowed in those days when one was serving in the Royal Navy. A wise ruling, of course, though I cannot help noticing how many seem to have benefited through disobeying it.

William van Narvig: that was the name of the clue which flashed through my mind. I remembered the Narvig part of the name because I had associated it with Narvik, the Norwegian port around which so many fierce naval battles were fought by the British and Germans in 1940. I recalled that I had met him at the Hotel Pierre in New York when I was in the company of some American journalists. It had seemed natural to me as a journalist to gravitate towards people working on American newspapers and so escape temporarily from brother officers who tended to 'talk shop'.

I was introduced to van Narvig by a character named Wythe Williams. Other American journalists had insisted that I 'must meet Wythe Williams ... he is the tops of his profession, probably the one man in America who knows more about what's going on in occupied Europe than anyone else.' So it was that when someone said, 'Come along to the Hotel Pierre tomorrow night and you will see Wythe,' I enthusiastically agreed. And with Wythe and, if I remember correctly, two other people, was the mysterious William van Narvig, known to Wythe as "Bill".

I still try to remember what he was like; it isn't easy. In the night life of New York the lights of many bars were so dim that one had no more than an impression of ghostlike figures, peering through the gloom. There was also the fact that after the fourth daiquiri, or the third whip cocktail (consisting of absinthe, French vermouth, brandy and curaçoa) all the faces in the joyous gloom resembled Thurber cartoons. Thus it was that van Narvig was simply recollected as someone probably tall (he was sitting down all the time I saw him), clean-shaven, with a dominant but not unusual face and what one might call a European-American accent. I have a vague feeling that he had some kind of a facial mark: it may have been a scar or a spot.

Wythe Williams, now a long forgotten name, was talked about a great deal in intellectual and media circles in the USA in the period 1938-42, partly on account of his newspaper articles, but mainly because of his remarkably accurate prophecies and assessments of the European scene in his thrice weekly broadcasts entitled *As the Clock Strikes*. Born in Meadville, Pennsylvania in 1881, he worked on various newspapers in Minneapolis and Milwaukee, then moved to London and in 1912 became a correspondent there for the *New York Times*. In 1913 he moved to Paris and covered World War I from 1914-17.

A benign, rotund and puckish figure, Williams was nevertheless a most persistent investigative journalist in an age when that type of journalism was rare. Correspondents were not wanted at the front in World War I, censorship was inexorable and sometimes they were locked up on suspicion of being spies. Once he evaded the authorities and made his way into the French trenches at Verdun. 'You will never get there,' he was told by a French officer. 'The Germans have their *tir de barrage* going full force.' Through mud holes and over craters, at times stumbling over dead men, with shells flaming and booming all around, Williams managed to get a tremendously descriptive and impressive story.

In 1918 he was special correspondent for *Collier's Magazine* in Europe and the next year for the London *Daily Mail* in Berlin. After a spell as director of propaganda for the American Committee for Devastated France, he rejoined the *New York Times* in 1927 as special correspondent at the League of Nations in Geneva. His reputation was by this time so high that he was elected President of the Association of Journalists accredited to the League. In 1929 he spent some time as a correspondent in Berlin and in the early thirties covered most of the various disarmament conferences, becoming thoroughly disillusioned by what he saw as the lack of realism on the part of the Western democracies.

As a result of this Williams decided to try almost single-handedly to educate these same democracies to the stark facts of life as he saw them. He ran into trouble in 1929 during a US Senate inquiry into alleged influence of armaments interests in the Geneva Naval Conference held in 1927. Senator William B. Shearer, admittedly violently anti-British and styled as the man who wrecked the conference, was alleged to have had correspondents and naval officers at the conference on his payroll. Williams and others mentioned by the big-navy advocate denied the charges and nothing came of them.

In 1937 Williams became editor of *Greenwich Time* in Connecticut and soon provided that modest suburban daily newspaper with a series of quite astonishing world scoops, as well as establishing for himself a reputation as a prophetic news analyst and radio commentator. Meanwhile he criticised the futilities of the League of Nations and warned about the inevitability of war when virtually no one in the democracies considered it as a possibility. This lesson he tried to hammer home in a book, *The Dusk of Empire*, possibly one of the most perceptive works of the day but largely dismissed by many reviewers.[1]

Things 'might have been quite different,' he argued, 'if the League of Nations ever presented the spectacle of international delegates honestly getting together. It never did.' It was his opinion that the world was not ready for the League in 1919 and that 'so long as mankind remains as it is, the world will not be ready for it.' He stressed that he was sceptical about the maintenance of peace, and that war lay ahead: '... the danger period will begin about Easter, 1937. From then on through the summer the spark leading to explosion may be ignited at any hour.' Then, in an effort to arouse his countrymen out of the isolationist day dreams, he added in more enthusiastic mood: 'The first place in the sun is today open to the United States. If it is occupied, then the world civilization may not only remain intact, but rise to a brilliance beyond imagination.'[2]

Readers were puzzled that so modest a newspaper could produce so many scoops from such far distant places. Lowell Thomas, the author of *With Lawrence in Arabia* and himself a radio commentator of influence, wrote of Williams that he 'had been one of the ace reporters of the European scene. When he earned that reputation he got his stuff with the formidable machinery of the foreign service of the *New York Times*, of the Northcliffe Press and the United Press at his back. After he returned from Europe he had apparently nothing but the slender resources of *Greenwich Time* ... From his desk in Greenwich, Connecticut, Wythe proceeded to pull one news rabbit after another out of his hat. He had us not only guessing, but more than slightly sceptical. How could one man, we asked, dig up information not available to the great newspapers who had their own news-gathering machinery? So some of us looked upon the beats that Wythe was scoring with raised eyebrows. But, by jingo, history began to vindicate and corroborate him.'[3]

The link-man in Wythe Williams' epic-making scoops was none other than the character who called himself Captain William van Narvig, though Williams admitted much later that that was not his real name. As I understood it from both men it was essential that his real identity was kept secret, otherwise he would not have been able to wander all around Europe with impunity. Of his conversation I recall only a little: he was a listener rather than a talker on this occasion. But what he said was very much to the point. 'America would be in a much stronger position today,' he said, 'if the government had adopted Wythe's idea for creating a great army and navy and, by introducing short-term conscription, providing a trained force of one million men way back in 1937. That might have made some people in Europe hesitate about plunging us into war.' I do remember that he quietly insisted that when World War II ended, the result would be quite different from that which most people expected. Hitler would go, yes, but in his place would appear a new and even more powerful enemy in Stalin's Russia.

Not long after this meeting my ship was completed and ready to be taken over at Philadelphia and, sailing down the Delaware Canal to Norfolk, Virginia, and from there via Bermuda, my flat-bottomed landing-craft eventually reached Gibraltar and entered the war in North Africa. It was many years later that I recalled the name of William van Narvig and began to look into his career.

Suddenly in the late 1960's I was lured into writing about espionage, and in particular in writing a history of the British secret service down the ages. It was then I recalled something that van Narvig had said which had meant very little to me at the time. He had spoken briefly about one of the most remarkable of British secret agents in modern times, a man who called himself Sidney Reilly. I had quite frankly thought he was talking rubbish, largely because at that time the name Sidney Reilly meant very little to me, except for the fact that he was said to have been killed by Soviet guards in September 1925 when he tried to smuggle himself into Russia from Finland.

Trying to reconstruct what he had said, as far as my memory would serve me, I cited for my *History of the British Secret Service* (published in 1969) the following remarks by van Narvig: 'There is no question at all that Reilly did not know he was entering a wolves' lair. He was fully aware that the Trust (this was an organization that claimed it would help to bring anti-Bolsheviks back into power in Russia) was a cover for Russian counter-espionage agents. But Reilly was a changed man after 1922. He was disgusted that the British Secret Service had become pro-German. It was that which made him change his attitude towards the Soviet, though it did not, unhappily, cause the Soviet to change its attitude towards him. Ever since Reilly was captured the Russians have had two of their own agents inside the British Secret Service.'[4]

Much of Reilly's story has been romanticized in films and the narratives of other people. In his time he had worked as a spy for the British, for Czarist Russia, Japan and the United States, and, so some allege, even the Chinese, though I find the latter suggestion largely unproven. Subsequent information has tended entirely to support van Narvig's comments on Reilly. In June, 1966, the journal, *Nedelya*, gave a Russian version of the fate of Sidney Reilly. This admitted that he had been lured back into Russia by The Trust, but claimed that he was captured and held in custody, rather than shot at the border. The article stated that on 13 October 1925, Reilly wrote to Dzerzhinsky, head of the *Cheka*, saying he was ready to cooperate and to give full information on the British and American Intelligence Services.[5]

Then in 1987 Mr Robin Lockhart, son of the British diplomat who knew Reilly and had worked with him, lent further credence to van Narvig's assertions. In the preface to a second book on this subject Mr Lockhart stated: '... there were those in the intelligence community who considered Reilly to be an adventurous scoundrel who had probably ultimately thrown in his lot with the Soviets to save his skin. Much more to the point were the views of some of the hierarchy in MI 5.... who believed that Reilly was "The First Man" to have defected. There was abundant circumstantial evidence to show that it was Reilly who had paved the way for Burgess, Maclean, Philby, Blunt et al.'[6]

When I published some of the comments I recalled van Narvig having made, some people in security circles became interested and asked me to tell them more about the man. There was not a great deal I could tell and by that time Wythe Williams, with whom I had kept in touch, was dead. But I remembered another comment of van Narvig's which in the late 1960's seemed relevant even though in 1942 I had tended to disregard it. That comment was: 'There was never any chance that the Soviet Union would make any agreement with Britain when talks began in the early summer of 1939. They knew that in the British Foreign Office and the Secret Service were men of influence who were predominantly anti-Bolshevik and pro-German. They knew because of what their own agents inside both the FO and the SIS told them. They knew perfectly well that these forces would like nothing better than to see Germany and Russia engaged in war while Britain and France looked on from behind the Maginot Line.'

It was at this stage that I began to become interested in the question of who William van Narvig really was. This interest was further stimulated by a friend of mine who had served in French Intelligence. He said to me: 'Who is this van Narvig? I think you should make a big effort to find out, as, undoubtedly from what you tell me, he could well have the answers to many questions which are puzzling us even today. One wonders, too, if the Americans have forgotten him. If so, they made a big mistake.'

Shortly after this I discovered that a great deal of intelligence about German military moves and dispositions and changes in the Nazi hierarchy was obtained both by the Allies and some others who were feeding information through the Soviet-controlled "Lucy" ring in Switzerland, through a mysterious character known for code purposes as "Walter" or "Werther." He also had the *nom de guerre* of Captain van Narvig. Could this be the same man as Wythe Williams' friend and correspondent? Further inquiries suggested that he very probably was that man. "Walter", or van Narvig, I was told had been an officer in the Russian Imperial Army; he was not really a Russian, however, but one of that cosmopolitan band from whom secret agents are so readily recruited, having been born in St Petersburg of an English mother and a German father, while he himself was a citizen of Finland.

But the irritating thing was that I knew prefectly well that van Narvig was not his real name. Wythe Williams had assured me that it was not and he claimed to have known the man since World War I. I wrote to *Greenwich Time*, the paper which Williams had edited, and sought information there. Then I discovered a man named Bernie Yudain who had been a young reporter on *Greenwich Time* when Wythe Williams arrived to take over the paper. We corresponded and this is what he told me:

'Van Narvig, I'm sorry to say, I never heard of in the time-frame he was allegedly working with Williams. Alas, there are few around from that era. But undoubtedly Williams and van Narvig between them pulled off some amazing scoops. What bugs me is the expense of running an operation such as Williams described. No way could he have helped finance such an operation and there seems no suggestion that van Narvig was a man of private means. Certainly Williams did not get financed by his radio sponsors. So who provided the funds?'

Mr Yudain seemed to think that there might be a clue to the identity of van Narvig in a Dutch writer named Henrik Wilhelm van Loon who frequently wrote pieces for *Greenwich Time*. He had been a leading figure in the anti-Nazi crusade in Connecticut and had written an item which stated: 'Finally the war broke out and the quiet Ivory Tower of this historical recluse became a madhouse. Finnish relief work brought Finns and Swedes and Norwegians. Dutch relief work brought other queer guests. These were the usual literary pilgrims and drove of refugees from many lands ...'

It was soon obvious that van Loon could not have been van Narvig. By this time Bernie Yudain had begun to suspect that Williams had invented van Narvig, creating a character who sounded romantic and all-knowing. But then another possible candidate in Wythe Williams' circle emerged: one Fritz Max Cahen, a German-Jewish refugee from Hitler. At one time he worked in the German Foreign Office as personal secretary to Count Brockdroff-Rantzau. It was Cahen who handed over to Wythe Williams the first final draft of the Versailles Treaty after World War I, giving the American a world-wide scoop which was one of his greatest boasts throughout his life.

Mr Yudain said that Cahen was between the wars 'involved in anti-Nazi underground work in several countries, always fleeing just as the Nazis were taking over. Shortly after Williams arrived at Greenwich in October 1937, Cahen showed up. He was, in my opinion, a principal source of Williams' information. He scratched out a living, I know not how because if Williams gave him anything, at best it would have been a pittance. It would seem that Williams picked up van Narvig just as the Cahen connection was ending: there was a falling-out between the two men.[7]

It was clear that sometime early in 1940 inquiries were being made in Washington by the British about Fritz Max Cahen. A classified and confidential memorandum from the Department of State, concerning a request by Captain Guy Liddell, of Britain's MI 5, stated: 'Reference is made to H.V.J. (Herschal V. Johnson Counsellor at US Embassy in London) memorandum no. 63 of 6 July 1938, in which information was requested with regard to Fritz Max Cahen, also known as Ferdinand Max Cahen. It is understood that Mr Cahen is now residing in Greenwich, Connecticut, and that he is a close friend of Wythe Williams who publishes the *Greenwich Time* and who was formerly a well-known foreign correspondent in Europe. No information has been developed to show that he is pro-Soviet, but he has been reported to be decidely anti-Nazi. Conflicting information has been received with regard to him personally. Some consider him to be very egotistical and likely to exaggerate his importance. Mr Williams, however, is said to believe in him, and it is his interest which is said to have given Cahen some standing.'[8]

The report also confirmed Cahen's work as secretary to Count Brockdroff-Rantzau. But it led one no nearer to the identity of van Narvig. One had to admire Wythe Williams for having kept the secret of his ace informant so well. The reason for this he gave in a book which he wrote with van Narvig in 1943. 'When we wrote this book in the early months of 1942,' he stated in the preface, 'it was to bring home to American readers the full depth of sinister forces that arrayed themselves against the life, liberty and pursuit of happiness of the common man. The average American mind was confused on the real significance of events, and even fearful to some extent. We believed that by revealing certain secrets that had come to our knowledge through a stroke of good fortune, we might be able to contribute to the dispersion of some of this confusion.... The price America has to pay for her unpreparedness is heavy. It will grow heavier still.... the question will be asked, how was it possible for our informants to get access to all the secret information?. . . . They could move freely in places where secret schemes were concocted. They were unsuspected. . . . The very nature of their revelations demands that their actual names and positions remain undisclosed for the time being. . . . To be found opposed to Nazi designs, or even suspected of such opposition, means the end. Moreover, information useful to American authorities continues to flow through these same channels. The sources of this information must be protected.

'Perhaps the most difficult task in compiling this book was to present the facts so as to eliminate all clues pointing to the actual sources. It entailed a considerable amount of juggling by the authors. The various reports had to be edited most carefully. On occasions the dates and places had to be shifted. . . . Some reports had to be omitted in their entirety, as they would unmistakeably have pointed at their source.'[9]

But this only whetted my enthusiasm for the task of finding out more about van Narvig.

THE QUEST FOR VAN NARVIG

About this time my quest for van Narvig switched from the USA to Finland. It did seem as though he might well have been an officer in Marshal Mannerheim's army against the Bolsheviks after the Russian revolution. I had been briefly in touch with Wythe Williams after World War II and, while he was not forthcoming about who van Narvig really was, he hinted that he had contacts high up inside Soviet Intelligence and that, with the "Cold War" continuing, it was important that his identity should remain secret. Indeed, for a while I began to wonder whose side van Narvig was on, whether all the time he had been helping the Russians against the Germans and was still in touch with them, or if he had merely infiltrated Soviet ranks.

Then I read what Whittaker Chambers, the most literate of the apostate Soviet agents, had said about a Soviet agent named "Willi". Willi was six feet tall, later he called himself "Bill" (like van Narvig) and he was either Esthonian or Finn. 'He [Willi] took me away from Peters [his other Soviet contact], put me in his own Soviet underground apparatus. I used to meet him once a week ... Bill's chief project was to set up a Soviet apparatus in England. This use of the US as a base for establishing Soviet apparatuses in other countries was then a common practice. I had been selected to assist Bill in London. He instructed me to provide myself at once with a business "cover" — an American firm that would send me to represent it in London. I must provide myself with papers on which I could secure a fraudulent passport. I was to organize a courier system. Suddenly this plan went dead.'[1]

Not much came from following up the case of "Willi" the

Finn. But I did receive unstinting help from Finland in my quest. This came from Jukka Rislakki of Helsinki, who was researching for a book about Finnish Intelligence which was eventually published as *Erittäin salainen — Vakoilu Suomessa* (*Top Secret — Spying in Finland*). He, too, was interested in the mysterious "Werther" or "Walter" or "William van Narvig".

He reported to me that, according to Finnish sources, the man 'used the name "Werther" in Switzerland when he helped the network there. It is said that there was a Finnish woman there, too, and that she had a clandestine radio set during the war years.'[2]

Jukka Rislakki added: 'If you take a look at Hans Rudolf Kurz's book, *Nachrichtenzentrum Schweiz*, you find that there were two agents whose real names were never discovered. They were "Werther" and "Olga". "Werther" was a very important part of the network and there has been a lot of speculation as to his identity.'[3]

Between us we pursued several possible candidates for the role of van Narvig. Two names immediately suggested themselves as worthy of further investigation. One was Lieutenant-Colonel John William Rosenbroijer, born at Schuwalovo in 1887, who had an English mother and who died in the 1950's; but nothing in his career fitted into the pattern of van Narvig's life. Another was Edvin Bertel Rosenbroijer, who was born in Baku, Russia, in 1887, and who had been Mannerheim's staff officer as well as being adjutant to the President of Finland and the head of the foreign department (military intelligence) of the Finnish General Staff. But careful checking showed no American links and certainly not any indication of the man in question having adopted American nationality.

Was it possible that at some date the brothers Rosenbroijer could have loaned their personal data to "van Narvig" so that the one could impersonate the other. But once again there was no evidence to support this theory. Other names turned up, among them Walter von Gerich, who had been Mannerheim's *aide-de-camp* for a long time. A Finnish general gave his opinion that von Gerich "fitted" van Narvig and he was sure they were one and the same. Apparently von Gerich was a saboteur somewhere in the Murmansk area in the early 1920's working for British Intelligence. He had been born in 1881, but there seemed to be a mystery as to when he died. The first date given came from the official church certificates which stated that he died on 1 September 1935, in Helsinki. Then the archives of *Helsingin Sanomat* produced a surprising piece of evidence. In September 1939 (repeat 1939, not 1935) there was a small news item about a mysterious accident near Helsinki. It was reported that a car which did not stop, and which got away without being caught, hit Major Walter von Gerich as he was walking and that the major died in a Red Cross hospital. There was a police request for information on the car.

That was the only clipping in the newspapers. There was no further information about the accident, or a funeral. Was it possible that someone decided this was the day on which von Gerich should disappear — to re-emerge under another name? It was this possibility which prompted me to inquire of Sir William Stephenson, head of British Intelligence in the USA in World War II, whether he could throw any light on van Narvig. His cabled reply was: 'Repeat no trace van Narvig.'[4]

By this time I was almost on the point of giving up my quest for van Narvig, when I recalled what Bernie Yudain had said — 'obviously your research establishes there *was* a van Narvig, which puts to rest a sneaky suspicion in my mind that he could have been an invention.'[5]

I must confess that I myself had begun to think that Mr Yudain's "sneaky suspicion" was well founded. Yet I always came back to the fact that I had been introduced to van Narvig, or at least to someone claiming his name, while Wythe Williams had himself written about him in some detail, even though he was careful to conceal almost any clue that might lead to his being identified. Since Wythe Williams was dead, and could not answer any further queries, I carefully studied the notes I had made, partly from memory and partly from the few letters I had had from Wythe Williams after the war. One interesting point that Williams had made was that van Narvig had insisted he 'owed a lot to Sidney Reilly': this was in answer to a query of mine about what I recalled van Narvig saying at that meeting in New York. 'Van Narvig told me that it was Reilly who taught him that the best spy was a freelance agent, a precept which he had always followed up.'[6]

Van Narvig had also claimed to be 'partly responsible for the defection of Walter Krivitsky, the Soviet Intelligence chief in Europe, in 1937, to Canada and the USA.' According to van Narvig, Krivitsky knew how and by whom British Intelligence had been penetrated by the Russians. I recalled that van Narvig had claimed that the British Foreign Office and Secret Service were anti-Bolshevik and pro-German. True in 1939 there were still elements of appeasement inside the British establishment and these were sometimes anti-Soviet as well, but this still seemed to me to be a massive exaggeration and applicable only to a few people. Was van Narvig being fed with disinformation from someone inside the British camp? Or was it possible, I wondered, that van Narvig was actually an under-cover Soviet agent, despite all the suggestions that he fought against the Bolsheviks?

Wythe Williams had replied briefly that he felt sure van Narvig was not playing a pro-Soviet game at this time, though he agreed this could not be entirely ruled out.

'If he had any motives at all, it seemed to me that he wanted to alert the United States to the fact that there were two enemies, who, sooner or later, they would have to fight — Germany and Japan. At no time did he suggest that Soviet Russia was a trustworthy ally. But I do recall that twice he gave some information which hinted at pro-German intrigues in London. The first was some kind of plot to use the Duke of Windsor as an intermediary for a patched-up peace and calling off of war plans, and the second item of information he described as "so red hot that you simply must not use it, as it could cause appalling damage." This was that van Narvig had had on the most reliable authority that in the middle of August, 1939, negotiations had been established between Marshal Goering and the head of the British Secret Service for Goering to make a secret visit to London for peace talks with Chamberlain.'

Wythe Williams also added that he believed van Narvig was a close acquaintance of Colonel Josef Veltjens, who was Goering's right-hand man. This last statement reminded me that a Finnish lieutenant-colonel named Bertel Efraim Martenson, who was born in 1893, had also had business deal-ings with Colonel Veltjens who arranged arms for Finland. But the chance that Martenson might have been van Narvig, or vice versa, faded when I discovered that he had been arrested by the Germans during World War II and had died in Ravensbruck prisoners-of-war camp in April 1945. Martenson did not speak English and was never in the USA, and van Narvig was still alive long after 1945.

On the other hand a search in the British Public Records office revealed some astonishing confirmation of van Narvig's claims. This is contained in the British Foreign Secretary's (Lord Halifax's) personal *Record of Events Before the War, 1939*. The entry for 21 August stated:

'Went to the Office early and to No. 10 at 11.30 with Alec [then Lord Dunglass, Parliamentary Private Secretary to the Prime Minister, Neville Chamberlain, and today Lord Home] to see the PM. A general discussion of all possibilities and probabilities and approved the letter to Hitler. "C" [head of the SIS, Admiral Sinclair] tells us that he has received an approach suggesting that Goering should come over to London if he can be assured that he will be able to see the Prime Minister. It was decided to send an affirmative answer to this curious suggestion, and arrangements were accordingly set in hand for Goering to come over secretly on Wednesday the 23rd. The idea is that he should land at some deserted aerodrome, be picked up by car and taken direct to Chequers. There the regular household is to be given *congé* and the telephone to be disconnected. It looks as if it is going to be a dramatic interlude, and, having laid the plans, we await confirmation from Germany.'[7]

After Wythe Williams' death in 1958 at the age of seventy four, it was for a long time impossible to obtain any further clues about van Narvig. It was only gradually, during the late sixties and then throughout the seventies, that I found oblique references to this apparently phantom figure to encourage me to open a file on van Narvig. This was partly due to the fact that some Intelligence and Security officers over here suddenly became interested in what little I had written about the man and were anxious to have my own account of my meeting with him.

In my personal quest for van Narvig's real identity it seemed first of all essential to sift out any disinformation which Wythe

Williams himself might have served up on van Narvig to cover up his real identity. To me personally Wythe Williams had written: 'Of course, turning out that book so that we could give readers a worthwhile and authentic narrative and at the same time protect our sources — not only from arrest by the Gestapo, but, in van Narvig's case, from arrest by the NKVD, too, was very difficult. Apart from that there was the over-riding question of the national interest in wartime. Despite the fact that war is now long since over, the cold war is very much with us and so van Narvig still needs much the same kind of protection.'[8]

The question was how to recognize any disinformation William's had introduced into his picture of van Narvig. Could it be, for example, that the man was not a Finn, and had not fought in the Russian Imperial Army? Instead, could he be an Austrian who had fought in the Spanish Civil War, or a Hungarian who had taken American citizenship? Or could it be that the mystery man was really a Russian who had defected from the Soviet Union, possibly shortly before World War II? I recalled that in one of his letters Wythe Williams had referred to some information which van Narvig had obtained from a high Soviet source and that van Narvig 'very much doubted some of this and suspected that it was intended for him to sow seeds of mistrust between America and Britain.'

There also seemed to be a Swiss connection, not merely from information obtained from Finland, but from "Roger", the code-name of a pre-war Soviet apparat in Switzerland. "Roger" has kept clear of all espionage entanglements for a long time, to the best of my knowledge, and is totally dis-illusioned about the USSR, but for his own safety his identity still needs to be kept secret. "Roger" agreed that there had been a Finn active in Switzerland during the war: 'He was in and out of the country and he spoke English as well as German and French. But his code-name was "Werther" not "Walter". I'm sure it is the same man and that someone had confused the code-name. Now there was at this time an order that "Werther's" identity was top secret and, as far as I know, none of us on the fringes of the underground networks in Switzer-land at this time ever knew who "Werther" really was. Roessler knew his identity and so, too, did Sandor Rado, but

16

they are both dead. "Werther" had an equally top secret female agent whose code-name was "Olga". She was also Finnish, was supposed to have escaped from Germany at some time or other and had a clandestine radio set."[9]

This information from "Roger" seemed to tie in with what van Narvig had passed on to *Greenwich Time* in some of his reports. In researching the story of the "Lucy" Ring for my *History of the British Secret Service*, I gathered that a good deal of additional intelligence on Germany was obtained by the Soviet Swiss network from the material which "Werther" or "Walter" had passed through to it. It was also clear from the work of Pierre Accoce and Pierre Quet in their book, *La Guerre a été gagnée en Suisse*, that Rudolf Roessler, one of the chief contributors to the "Lucy" network, had contacts in Switzerland.

"Roger's" tip-off made even more sense when I studied one report early in World War II which Wythe Williams received in a series of letters from van Narvig from various parts of the globe. This particular report bore a Rio de Janeiro postmark and van Narvig had apparently found some way of sending it to Brazil by a plane of the Italian-operated Lati line to South America, thus avoiding censorship. It spoke of events in Europe and stated:

'There is a second party — Clara. Clara's position is such that she has access to virtually all the documents that are executed by Hitler — I should have said rather, their copies — or that pass through the executive and secretarial offices at the Berghof ... She, too, has good reason to hate the ruling Nazis. In 1934 Clara fell in love. The man was an aide to Captain Roehm [Ernst Roehm, head of the Stormtroopers who was purged in the blood bath on 30 June 1934] and she saw him frequently at the Berghof. They were married.... secretly. Hardly a month later the Roehm faction was purged and Clara's husband was among those killed.... Presently Clara knew she was to have a baby. As she dared not reveal the identity of the father, she obtained a leave of absence and went to Switzerland where her child was born.'

Soon it became clear that "Clara" and "Olga" were almost certainly code-names for the same person. Van Narvig had a Swiss bank account and was able to finance her in dollars while she provided him with funds in Germany. After seeing her child safely settled in Switzerland, "Clara" returned to Germany for a while and contributed admirable intelligence for van Narvig. One day she received a hand-delivered note which read: 'You are no longer safe at your home or at the Berghof. Go immediately to B----.' It was a signal that van Narvig's German network was beginning to break up. Shortly after this van Narvig had a letter which told him that 'Clara is safe in Switzerland ... Gottlieb was very good in that his help to Clara is admirable. If we go into Russia it may be difficult to transmit my letters to Gottlieb. Therefore if you do not hear from me for sometime, do not think that I am not working with you.'[10]

Obviously all these names were aliases, and all the time I had to beware of disinformation, put out to keep the enemy in the dark, and to overcome simple lack of information. Even when the war was ended, and for some years afterwards — in fact right up to the time of his death — Williams remained reticent, largely on the grounds that van Narvig was still alive and still moving in and out of territories where he was 'liable to arrest, if his true identity was known,' and that the same applied to some of the other sources. Gottlieb, who arranged the escape of Clara from Germany to Switzerland, had actually been a member of the Gestapo. Van Narvig wrote of him at the time that he came from a well-to-do Bavarian family: 'he is a Gestapo man — that is, he is in the Gestapo, but not of it. Many of the Berghof staff are Gestapo agents whose duty it is to spy on those close to Hitler .... Gottlieb is one of those men.'

My other contact in Helsinki was convinced that, while most of the background information about van Narvig was accurate, there must have been sufficient disinformation cleverly combined with it to put his enemies right off the trail of his identity. As this contact, whom I shall call "Soloist", is an authority on intelligence matters, I accept this viewpoint. 'I am beginning to wonder if van Narvig's father had Finnish nationality and was not German at all,' he wrote. 'Could he have been in the lumber business and not in the Army? Maybe we have been looking in the wrong places. If he was ever in the lumber business in Karelia, he must have known the Com-

munist business-woman and writer, Hella Wuolijoki, a friend
of Brecht. She was thought to have been an agent either of the
British Secret Service, or the USSR, or both. During the war
she was in prison.'

Persistent inquiries all around Europe, Russia and the USA
eventually produced some positive results. I managed to track
down a number of the articles which van Narvig had written
for the American press after World War II which provided
information in his own words. Then, and in some ways this was
the most vital of all, I obtained a photograph of van Narvig
through the courtesy of the *New York Times*. The same newspaper also had in its possession an autobiographical statement
by van Narvig, in his own handwriting, dated "April 1936".

This revealed that William van Narvig was the pen-name of
William Otto Lucas, an American citizen and president of the
American Writers' Association. His statement indicated that he
wrote and spoke 'five principal languages fluently,' that he
read 'nine additional languages, had travelled three times
round the world, had visited every country in the northern
hemisphere, was forty three years old, six feet two inches tall.' I
can only assume from the way in which this statement was
written that William Lucas (to give him his American name)
was seeking journalistic assignments, for he mentioned having
'reverted to writing articles on economic subjects, short stories,
a novel — the latter still unpublished — and numerous baseball
stories, which, if anything, prove my one hundred per cent
Americanization.'

Briefly, this statement confirmed in part what Wythe
Williams had said about van Narvig — that he was born in St
Petersburg of a German father and a British mother, with the
additional information that his father had been conductor of
the Russian Imperial Opera Company. But far more detail of
his life was given than had ever been hinted at by Wythe
Williams, or published in the book, *Secret Sources*. After graduating at Riga University Lucas spent five years in the employ of
the General Electric Company and supervised the construction
of the street car system in Archangel and Samara in Russia, as
well as conducting a survey of the water power resources in
North Russia and the Upper Volga Basin. This work was done
under the auspices of the Imperial Industrial Commission.

During the same period he contributed articles on engineering and rural electrification in various technical journals.

In August 1914, Lucas was drafted for active military service, but details of this are confusing and puzzling. Wythe Williams, who met him during World War I, said he was 'an officer of the Russian Army ... He was actually a citizen of Finland, and after graduating from a Russian University, had entered the army with the rank of lieutenant.' Lucas himself makes no mention of any Finnish citizenship at this period in any of his signed statements on his career. His exact description of his joining up in World War II is that he 'served as lieutenant and captain in the Aviation Corps on the Carpathian front.[11] In a declaration to the Federal Bureau of Investigation, made through various sources during World War II, he stated that he 'was a Russian pilot in an old Curtis Special during World War I'.

He added that he was shot down early in 1915 on the Carpathian front, while directing the Russian artillery in the battle for Dukla Pass on an occasion when he was flying 'a rickety Farman pusher plane'. Enemy shrapnel ripped one of his plane's wings and he crashed inside his own lines. After months spent in field hospitals he was appointed a member of the Russian Government Purchasing Commission in the United States, presumably because of his technical and engineering knowledge and his command of several languages.

Then comes this surprising statement by Lucas: 'Seeing a profitable opportunity for going into business on my own, I resigned my post in October, 1915, to establish an export firm under the name of W.O. Lucas and Company, at 18 South La Salle Street, Chicago, and at 17 Battery Street, New York, at the same time setting up engineering and sales offices in Petrograd and Moscow, dealing in machine tools and motor trucks.' That a serving officer in the middle of a world war could resign his post to start a business is almost beyond belief. One can only imagine that Lucas persuaded the authorities that it was in the interests of their obtaining supplies that he should do so.

To some extent this surmise seems to have been borne out by Lucas's further claim that, late in 1916, he was appointed a member of the Commission for the Mobilisation of Private Industry, and by September 1917 he stated that he had raised the output of his plant to forty cars a day and 'my enterprise in the United States and Russia gave employment to more than 2,500 people.'[12]

3

WYTHE WILLIAMS' STORY

At last two names tied up — van Narvig and Lucas. What was more, the latter name was documented within official sources. But these, while useful, gave very little detail of William Otto Lucas in the years leading up to World War II.

I was by now satisfied that this must have been the man to whom I was introduced in August, 1942, but I needed to check Lucas's story with what Wythe Williams had revealed about van Narvig. On the whole Williams' introductory narrative on van Narvig tallied with that given by Lucas in his statement of 1936, though it was, of course, much less detailed. According to Williams, the two men met in July 1915, when the former was a correspondent for the *New York Times*, accredited to the French Army. The man he described as Captain William van Narvig, a Russian Army officer, called at his office and asked if he could look through the files of the New York papers. Williams recalled that he did not drink vodka, but had a preference for Scotch and soda. Up to this point what Lucas told Williams tallied entirely with Lucas's biographical notes for the *New York Times* twenty years later. But Williams still seemed to be hinting at Finnish citizenship without giving any reasons for this.

'A decoration he wore aroused my curiosity,' said Williams. 'He confessed that he had received it for doing something or other over Austrian artillery positions in Galicia.' It was then that Lucas told Williams that his mission was with the Russian Purchasing Commission for acquiring equipment from the USA. He also ruefully told Williams that there was so much graft, inefficiency and indolence in the Purchasing Commission that 'the amount of money they get away with each month would equip a Russian division.' This statement alone suggests how Lucas was able to resign his post and open up a business dealing in arms for the Russians, probably much more efficiently than if he had remained in the Army.

What most impressed Williams then was Lucas's ability to look into the future. Lucas had already come to the conclusion that the most important thing about the armies of the future was that they would move on wheels and their striking power would be that much greater. Later Williams learned that Lucas had obtained a subsidy from the Russian government to build his own automobile plant.

For a while the two men corresponded. Then came the Russian revolution and Williams heard that Lucas's factory had been taken away from him. The last letter he had from him reported that Lucas intended to make his way to South Russia to join the volunteer army of 'my friend, General Kornilov.' This was after he had announced that he was on the staff of General Gustav Mannerheim in Finland. Here then was a discrepancy: Lucas had made no mention of this in his other statements, and "Soloist" reported from Helsinki that 'van Narvig must have been really in a hurry if he served both Kornilov and Mannerheim. Kornilov's army fought from December 1917 to April 1918, and Mannerheim founded his staff in Finland around February 1918 and conquered Helsinki in April 1918. Mannerheim left his post the following month.'

It is worth noting that General Kornilov was killed at the very beginning of the Civil War in Russia and that if Lucas fought with the anti-Bolshevik forces in this war, it would have been under Denikin or Yudenich or Wrangle, or some other anti-Bolshevik leader, and not Kornilov.

During the revolution in Russia Lucas and his family lost all their properties. In his autobiographical note of 1936 he claimed that he entered General Kornilov's volunteer Army as a divisional staff officer, and that he was taken prisoner by the Bolsheviks and spent 'five months and seventeen days in an Arctic prison camp; escaped four hours before my scheduled execution in January 1919, and reached the Finnish frontier in April, after a three-month trek through the Arctic wasteland.'[1]

Wythe Williams had mentioned receiving a letter signed 'William van Narvig, Lt.-Col., K.G.' He understood of course that the "K.G." stood not for Knight of the Garter, but for Knight of the Order of St. George, an Imperial Russian decoration. In his biographical notes, though, Lucas had made no reference to this decoration. Possibly Williams was attempting some discreet disinformation to make the identification of van Narvig more difficult. But it struck me as odd that, if Lucas was still so anxious to preserve a low profile and to hide his true identity, he should agree to have his photograph printed along with at least one of his articles. It occurred to me that the newspaper in question, the New York *Daily News*, might have obtained this photograph without his knowledge.

When I inquired of the New York *Daily News*, their very helpful chief librarian, Mr John C. Hodgson, replied that a search of their files had failed to turn up any personal information about van Narvig. Then he added this interesting statement: 'The photograph we used in our newspaper was taken by the Murnor Studio, 217 Aragon Avenue, Coral Gables, Florida. While checking the address of the studio in the Miami telephone directory I came upon the following:

Wm. Van Narvig, 8201 SW 41st Terrace,
Miami, Fla.
Telephone (305) 226 — 0376.
This was in a directory for 1978.[2]

The Murnor Studio, I discovered, had long since disappeared, but my contact in Miami reported: 'I had a long discussion with the Bell system long lines operator in Miami. Van dropped out of the phone book in 1980. He was able to check the number you provided and made a call to see if there was any spoor of Van. Regrettably, the new listing had nothing to contribute. Have asked a chum on the *Miami Herald* to do a search.'

But that later search, and others I organized, produced not one iota of a clue. The van Narvig cover-up still seemed to be working effectively.

From about 1917-18 onwards there was a long silence from Lucas, and this is all the more puzzling because it is clear that he had returned to the USA, and specifically to New York, on a number of occasions in the early 1920's. Why was it that he left it until June 1939 to get in touch with Williams? True, Williams had been in Europe for much of the time, but this would not have made all contact impossible. I make this point because there is some uncertainty about whether Lucas was helping Williams with information earlier than this. My own guess is that the true date of a meeting between the two could indeed have been much earlier.

The letter which Lucas sent in June 1939 was as follows:

'I understand that you have acquired the habit of taking cracks at the Mystic of Berchtesgaden. Beware! The fellow can bite, and right in this country, too. However, if you wear a bullet-proof vest and are interested in some real lowdown on your favourite subject, it is available. We met in an epoch which we called Armageddon. If you remember me, we might meet again.'[2]

Apparently the fact that the communication was signed "William van Narvig" made no sense to Williams. This suggests that way back in 1915-16 Williams had known the mysterious character by his real name of Lucas. Nevertheless, though he appeared not to have an idea who the person calling himself van Narvig was, he replied to the letter, albeit in a cautious way, and invited the writer to meet him at the Lotus Club in New York.

When they met, Williams recognized the man at once, and there began a lengthy association which led up to the series of scoops Williams achieved for *Greenwich Time* — which suddenly became very widely read for a suburban newspaper. Lucas made no secret of the fact that he had been in and out of the United States over many years, in Chicago, Detroit and New York, and that he was a supporter of the Brooklyn Dodgers baseball team. What astounded Williams was that Lucas used American slang in his talk. Lucas explained that he had taken United States citizenship and that he had made up his mind to 'become an American in every way that I know.'

It was from this stage onwards that Lucas began to open up on his life since he had first met Williams in the middle of World War I. After talking about his family and the need for settling down with new responsibilities, he mentioned that he was just back from his first trip abroad in many years, a ten-thousand mile journey through Russia to Siberia, then casually added that on his return he had paid a visit to Berchtesgaden.

This incidental information caused Williams to begin to take seriously this contact from the distant past. At last he saw Lucas as an ally and a correspondent. Lucas explained that he had a friend high up in the Soviet hierarchy whom he had helped escape "liquidation" during the Russian Civil War. It was this man who had made it possible for him to travel throughout the Soviet Union to the Crimea in the south and to Central Asia and Siberia in the north-east. But it was not the fact that Lucas was widely travelled which commended him to Williams so much as the fact that he had access to the Berghof, Hitler's mountain retreat in Bavaria. How he managed to gain access to this hide-out was obviously something Lucas needed to keep as top secret as his identity if he was to maintain his contacts there safely and still pass information to anti-Nazi papers in the Western world. Thus he sought out Williams, whom he had known, rather than more influential newspaper editors who not only wanted to know about him, but could not necessarily be trusted to keep such information to themselves.

There was another reason why Lucas preferred to deal with an experienced newspaper man such as Williams rather than with the major papers of the USA; this was that the two men shared a common desire to launch a crusade against Hitlerism and the dangers which threatened the Western world. Not only did Williams take Lucas's own view, that the democratic nations must sooner or later be prepared to fight Hitler, but he had already established himself as a very effective exponent of such views as a radio commentator. And this was the period in which, for the very first time, the radio commentator who could analyze the world news was coming into his own. Despite the theories of some that Lucas was a supporter of Soviet Russia (largely because he was able to go in and out of that country fairly easily) he was adamant that Stalin was more of an empire-builder than a genuine traditional Communist, and that he would not hesitate to make a deal with the Nazis. When this warning was borne out by the Nazi-Soviet pact of 1939, Lucas's reputation in the USA was greatly enhanced.

The apparently mysterious interval before Williams heard from Lucas in June 1939 can be discounted. This was a "cover-up", and it is probable that Lucas himself insisted on it because for at least two years previously he had been plying Williams with inside information from Europe and Russia.

Captain Guy Liddell, then in charge of "B" Division (counter-espionage) of MI5 in London, had been taking note of some of the Greenwich paper's scoops at this time and was trying to find out who the informant was, seeking information through Herschel V. Johnson of the US Embassy in the British capital.[4] Some people, including members of staff of *Greenwich Time*, thought that the informant was Fritz Max Cahen. But if one studies carefully some of the items published in *Greenwich Time* prior to June 1939, it seems obvious that Lucas, and only Lucas, could have been the source. Indeed, it is even possible that Lucas may have encouraged Williams to take on the job at *Greenwich Time* and to develop it in the way he did. Lucas for quite a long time had a home in Brooklyn where he had become an enthusiastic supporter of the Dodgers baseball club, frequently attending their matches. His daughter, Margared D. Lucas, had been born in Brooklyn in January 1927. Certainly it was Lucas alone who was responsible for so many of the paper's scoops over a number of years.

For a while contact between the two men seems always to have been either at some discreet rendezvous in New York (later even these meetings were abandoned as being unwise) or by specially delivered messages and post. Clearly, once World War II broke out and Lucas was on the move, communications threatened to become a problem, especially as there was censorship in Europe. Lucas had left New York in July 1939, giving Williams to understand that he would set up his own network of informants in certain key countries in Europe and that he would contrive by various methods to keep *Greenwich Time* posted. Williams was at first chagrined when he learned that Lucas had changed his plans and was leaving Hamburg for Moscow, but he understood the reason for this when his friend intimated the imminence of a German-Soviet Pact.

Wythe Williams duly recorded that 'although van Narvig had fought against the Bolsheviks, he had long since made his peace with the Soviets and had been aided by Z----ov in obtaining permission in 1938 to make an extensive tour of Russia.' Z----ov, 'whose full name cannot be told,' Williams then

27

explained, was a high Soviet official whom van Narvig had once saved from death.

This story of a freelance spy who could pop in to see Goering at Karin Hall, visit Hitler's hide-out at Berchtesgaden and also travel freely to Moscow seemed almost too good to be true. Was this disinformation, or was Lucas getting his intelligence from other people while claiming credit for doing the travelling himself? Certainly the intelligence obtained both in Russia and in Germany proved again and again to be one hundred per cent correct and his reports from Moscow were highly accurate.

Nevertheless for a long time I remained sceptical, like Bernard Yudain. I took the view that if I had written a spy novel and presented it to a publisher, using Lucas as my hero, he would reject the work on the grounds of sheer improbability. Another factor which puzzled me, just as it had Bernard Yudain, was the question of how Lucas's fact-finding was financed. Certainly *Greenwich Time* could not have afforded this, and, for that matter, few major United States daily newspapers could have done so. So, who found the money for these astonishing scoops involving, on occasions journeys across two continents.

After the war, Lucas, still using the pseudonym van Narvig, revealed a little more about himself in a series of newspaper articles. He confirmed the biographical statement that he had provided in 1936 for the archives of the *New York Times*. He also revealed the identity of Z----ov. It was none other than Andrei Alexandrovich Zhdanov, who had at one time been secretary-general of the Soviet Communist Party and heir apparent to Stalin. Lucas said that Zhdanov was an old friend: 'he shared the same bench with me in our school classroom. We were fellow officers in a crack regiment of the Imperial Guards that was almost annihilated in 1914 at Tannenberg. When he joined the Reds after the revolution and was captured, it was I who organized his escape.'[5]

When Lucas went to settle in the USA, the two men corresponded, whether openly or clandestinely is not clear. Then in 1934 Zhdanov invited his friend to visit him in Leningrad. At that time Zhdanov was the right-hand man of Sergei Kirov, ruler of the Leningrad district.

However, this statement by Lucas does not quite coincide

with the facts of Zhdanov's career. In all biographical entries on Zhdanov it is indicated that he joined the Bolsheviks in 1915, and that from 1924-34 he was head of the Communist Party organisation in Nizhni Novgorod, after which he went to Leningrad.

The most fascinating of all the Lucas — Wythe Williams mysteries at this period is the question of how Lucas obtained and communicated information on German signals traffic. If the story put out by Wythe Williams was disinformation, then one must assume that Lucas had means of obtaining details of German Army and Navy signals traffic either from inside Germany, or from a source in Switzerland. It could of course be that his sources were a mixture of both, otherwise it is impossible to explain why his intelligence proved to be so accurate. This applies as much to the Far East as to the Western world. One letter from Lucas to Williams in 1939 stated that, 'Our organization is growing. We've acquired two new converts, making four all told, with still a fifth in the offing. Our number three listening-post answers to the name of Wolfgang. The credit for enlisting him belongs to Clara.... Wolfgang works and lives at Fuschal Castle, near Salzburg ... It is a beautiful old estate which Joachim von Ribbentrop filched for himself.'

Williams told how in May 1940 Lucas came to New York, assembled a radio receiver and, having obtained the code, was able to decipher German signals.

'When, about noon on 8 May 1940, he [van Narvig] telephoned and asked that I come to his house.... I protested that I hadn't the time. He insisted. When I arrived van Narvig was on the roof, rigging up what seemed to me to be too much of an antenna. The receiving set I found to be a rather unimpressive black steel box.... The box seemed too small for the job it was intended to do and I had my doubts about its effectiveness.'[6]

Yet, despite these doubts, Lucas gave Williams a scoop that very night. He claimed to have decoded the message there and then, having obtained a copy of the German High Command ciphers some weeks before. Obviously, Lucas had realised that Williams' broadcasts, which started in January 1940, were beginning to have some effect in awakening Americans to the facts of life in Europe and elsewhere and stirring them out of their isolationist sloth. But Williams depended for these broadcasts on letters from Lucas which arrived haphazardly and from various addresses: he needed much more up-to-date intelligence and also to be sure that whatever he revealed would not put Lucas in danger.

If Williams was dubious about Lucas's radio set, the latter set him right when Williams suggested he could himself get a much more powerful set. 'It's not quite as easy as that,' was Lucas's response. 'There is the problem of the wavelengths. I know some of the wavelengths which the German General Staff uses for field communications, but I doubt very much if standard receivers are equipped to get them.'

Williams, according to his own account, watched while Lucas operated the controls, occasionally making notes with his pencil on a pad in front of him, apparently taking down the German in shorthand. Lucas said he had had to 'restudy this ancient Roller method of shorthand from Linda at Karin Hall,' adding that he had originally learned it as secretary to Walther Rathenau, the German Foreign Minister under the post-war republic, the man who not only signed the Rapallo Treaty but re-established relations with the USSR and was later killed by the Nazis.

Eventually he decoded what he told Williams was 'a scoop for your broadcast tonight.' The messages was to the effect that 'six army corps were moving up to the Dutch border from Papenburg in the north to Kleve in the south, while fourteen army corps were deploying towards the Belgian border between Aix-la-Chapelle and Daun, and four other corps were poised to move into Luxembourg.' On the basis of this intelligence Lucas estimated that the German armies would start moving into Holland within thirty six hours and into Belgium about the same time.

Prior to his broadcast that night Williams had a long argument with the radio station censor and administrator. The latter said that because no such information about German troop movements had come over the ticker tapes, the station could be accused of creating a false alarm if the news proved to be wrong. He said he needed to know where Williams was getting his information. Wythe replied that he could not reveal his contact. Eventually it was agreed that Williams might indicate that two German corps were on the move and that an invasion of the Low Countries seemed imminent.

This broadcast was made on the night of 8 May 1940. Two days later it was officially announced that the invasion of Belgium, Holland and Luxembourg had begun.

Nevertheless, despite this impressive scoop, one has to consider whether the story of Lucas listening in to, and deciphering the coded messages of the German High Command while he lived in New York was at least in part disinformation. Williams, of course, did not give any hint as to how he obtained his scoop: that was the main reason for the argument with the radio station censor. It was not until three years later that he told the story of the special set being built. Had such an incident been mentioned in 1940 it would have created something like panic in Whitehall, and even in the ranks of MI 5 and MI 6, as London was prepared to go to almost any lengths to keep quiet the fact that the British decoding team at Bletchley was reading German secret radio messages. And even in 1943, when *Secret Sources* was published, the British were still desperately anxious to maintain this secrecy. After all if Lucas, as an amateur spy, could manage to pull off such a scoop, it would be obvious to the Germans that all their communications were at risk.

One really needs to know not merely what Lucas's alleged 'special radio receiver' was like in much greater detail, but also what type of German military messages he was deciphering. Were they messages being sent from the USA to Berlin (from one or other of the German embassies or even a secret station), or were they messages being sent from inside Germany? If the former, then obviously a reasonably sophisticated short-wave receiver could have monitored direct communications from, say, the German Consulate-General in New York to Berlin. It is possible that Lucas could have gained some clues as to what was happening in German military circles from such messages, even through questions asked by the New York caller. To some extent the answer to this depends upon whether the Germans in such circumstances would use direct beam radio or the commercial telegraph circuits.

If, however, Lucas was listening in to messages emanating

from Germany, his receiver at that date would have had to be a massive affair with tall masts and aerials, something like the British sub-station of GCCS at Chicksands today. Irrespective of where the messages were coming from, they would have been in an Enigma key (the vital cipher which the British Secret Service had obtained shortly before World War II began). In effect that would mean that Lucas was claiming he had broken Enigma all by himself and possibly more than one key. But to believe this one would need to know the circuits he was intercepting. At this time Britains's deciphering boffins had no success with two main diplomatic keys, *Black Jumbo* and *Floradora*, so that makes one a little suspicious of Lucas's claims unless, of course, he had been given the key settings. There seems no doubt that there was some disinformation in this story.

On the other hand one has to consider this report on Lucas prepared for the Federal Bureau of Investigation in April 1944: 'While in Acalpulco the subject [i.e. Lucas] stated he was on a special mission for the U.S. War Department, having established German sources of information in 1939-40 in Berchtesgaden, Germany; intercepted announcement of French–German armistice in 1940 from Germany to the German military attaché, Madrid, effecting decipherment because he has copy of German Military Code.'[7]

This particular FBI report on Lucas also included information provided by the British SIS and there does not appear to have been any explanation from that side as to how Lucas secured the code, or got his information. Yet this single report suggests that Lucas must have impressed the Americans with his claims sufficiently to be welcomed as a new recruit for military intelligence.

What puzzled me in following up Williams' account of how Lucas was obtaining his intelligence was the fact that, though he carefully guarded his source in the early years, he allowed so much (admittedly under the code-name of van Narvig) to be told in 1943 when he published *Secret Sources*. Why, too, in view of Lucas's offer of his services to American Intelligence, was this book not drastically censored by the US Security Services? Or alternatively did these Services make some suggestions for disinformation?

As Bernard Yudain points out: 'When I was a reporter at *Greenwich Time*, it was my view and that of the few others on the staff who had the interest to care, that Fritz Max Cahen was the principal source of Williams' scoops. *Ergo*, van Narvig was never heard of by us. I never heard of the guy until I ran across the *Secret Sources* book. . . . how strange Williams rushed into print with it while the war was still on. One has to wonder why, and whether or not the entire action was not a piece of some more grand design of propaganda, or even disinformation.'[8]

"Roger" supplies another theory on Lucas's access to intelligence from Europe — that it was supplied by certain anti-fascist radio networks in Switzerland. 'I think the real answer to Lucas's alleged tapping of German High Command signals was that he was picking up information from Europe clandestinely radioed to him and that this may well have come from a member of the anti-fascist PAKBO organisation.'

But the story of PAKBO belongs to a future chapter.

4

WHAT THE RECORDS SAY

Slowly, some kind of a picture of William Otto Lucas is emerging, but the reader must still feel baffled. However, that is the way with spies who try to enter what for them might be called the Super Stakes. Even in the case of Sidney Reilly, it was very many years before he was finally unmasked as Sigmund Georgievich Rosenblum, the product of an illicit union between his aristocratic mother and a Jewish doctor from Vienna.

So far you have had my personal story of having met van Narvig/Lucas, some details from Wythe Williams, further information supplied by Lucas himself, and the theories of other people. It is all very intriguing, but it does not add up to a great deal. There is, of course, the photograph, but, though I met the man way back in 1942 in dimly lit premises in New York, I certainly would not like to swear on oath, more than forty years later, that this photograph was definitely that of the man I met. Put in a witness-box and carefully cross-examined, I should probably have to admit that the man I saw might have been a "cover" for someone else and that Lucas might not have been van Narvig after all.

Nevertheless, even at this early stage of the disentangling of the puzzle, it no longer makes sense — in the light of independent documentary evidence — to suggest that Lucas/van Narvig might be a fictional character.

It is worth considering just what official documentary records have to say on the subject of Lucas/van Narvig. Under the Freedom of Information Act in the USA certain papers concerning him have been released to the author. According to the Federal Bureau of Investigation, they hold the following files on Lucas/van Narvig: 'Internal Security 1940-1962, 600 pages; Internal Security 1973, 8 pages; Miscellaneous information, 60 pages.' This makes a total of 670 pages in all, not all of which have been released. It should perhaps be mentioned that, as a general rule, such papers concerning persons still living are not usually released and certainly not without the permission of the person concerned.

One of these documents states that 'Source B advised' [this was scratched out and it was substituted in writing 'It was learned'] 'that William Otto Lucas was born at St Petersburg [Leningrad] on 8 January 1893. His father was Otto Lucas, a German, and his mother was Caroline Yannutsch, of British nationality. He was naturalized as an American citizen in the year 1930. His occupation is that of a writer and his home address is 247 93rd Street, Brooklyn, New York. He is married to Margaret Marie Luthenheim. He is described as having white skin, brown eyes and brownish grey hair. He first arrived in Guatemala City at the Aurora airport on 28 October 1942, bearing the United States Special Passport No. 21402 [NB Special Passport]. He stayed at the Palace Hotel during that visit and gave as a reference the American Legation in Guatemala City. He advised that he had a Special Passport because he was a representative from the United States War Department, and Assistant Adjutant to the Assistant Military Attaché in Mexico City. On 28 February 1944, Lucas advised Source B [for some odd reason this name has been struck out of the record, thought it is still quite clear what the name of the source is] that he was in the Intelligence Service of the General Staff of the United States, and that he was working under the orders of Colonel Cruse. He gave as a reference on that date the --------' [here there is a total blackout on the name of the referee but as the word Guatemala follows the black-out one must assume it was someone stationed there.][1]

At the end of Lucas's report to the authorities stating that he had managed to decipher German military communications, there was an interesting comment, 'all information obtained in this report was obtained by the SIS [i.e. the British Secret Service]. Prior to making distribution of this report to outside ....ies, attention is called to the accompanying cover letter in .... to protect the identity of SIS [presumably the SIS source].' In other words both American and British Intelligence Services had some information on Lucas. This makes him much less of a phantom figure.

Apparently there had been some questioning of Lucas at this time, as another memorandum of that period states that 'in response to the question of how he obtained the German code, he replied that it was a secret.'[2]

Some few years later, after the war, there is a further official record on 'William Otto Lucas, also known as William van Narvig.' This stated that an examination of the records at the Hall of Records, Brooklyn, New York, revealed a deed recorded 27 May 1946, 'under the name of William Otto Lucas for the private dwelling located at 247 93rd Street, Brooklyn, New York. A mortgage on this property was recorded by the Bay Ridge Savings Bank, Brooklyn, New York.' This report went on to say that Lucas 'was also known by the pen-name of William van Narvig.' His age was shown as fifty-three, married, one dependent, and race American — Anglo.[3]

'American — Anglo' seems an odd way of describing Lucas, as the only alleged Anglo part of his ancestry was that of his mother. The report went on to say that Lucas's 'employment was shown as writer and author and that he had been employed in this line of work for the past twenty five years; that he was formerly connected with a number of newspapers as a feature writer; that during the past six or eight years he has turned to magazine work and also has turned out a rather well known book entitled *East of the Iron Curtain*, from which it is said that he is enjoying a profitable income. Lucas has the local respect and goodwill of neighbors in the immediate community. No derogatory legal information was set forth.'

One of Lucas's referees used by the FBI (whose name is erased from the released document) advised that he had 'known Lucas in a business way for the past ten years.' Another of the FBI's informants stated that he believed Lucas maintained a bank account at the National City Bank in the branch near his home. He further stated that Lucas had always met his financial obligations, 'but at times had been a little slow.'

Here then are some official records of checks made on
from a variety of sources, British as well as American,

the basis of these alone it can hardly be said any longer that he is some kind of fictional figure to provide a cover for Wythe Williams' informants. It was indeed on the basis of these reports that I began a world-wide quest for the elusive William Lucas, for elusive is the one adjective that permanently fits him. The ancient Japanese created a special kind of spy known as the *Ninja*, deriving from the word *ninjitsu*, which is defined as the 'art of making oneself invisible'; a *Ninja* was reputed to be able to walk on water, to appear and disappear at will and to obtain intelligence while 'invisible'. Lucas did better than that; he managed to disappear totally over long periods.

In assessing these various reports, it is necessary to bear in mind that the United States did not have a proper secret service until Roosevelt gave the go-ahead for the creation of the OSS in World War II. True, the FBI had been in existence for a long time and counter-espionage should therefore have been efficient, but it was often out of its depth coping with what can be termed 'secret service matters', though very successful in tackling straightfoward criminal problems. It depended very much upon information from the State Department on foreigners under surveillance, and the State Department in turn depended upon what its representatives abroad could discover. The British Secret Service reports on Lucas could not possibly have been a direct exchange of information between two friendly secret services; rather they followed a much more complex route from, possibly, Scotland Yard, MI 5 and the Foreign Office to the US Embassy in London, and from there to the FBI.

There is also evidence that, having accepted the information received on Lucas, the authorities appeared unhesitatingly to accept him as an officer in G-2 Military Intelligence in the USA when America came into the war on the side of the Allies against Germany and Japan. Yet the extraordinary thing is that, despite this, he and his family were still kept under observation by the FBI. One report states that 'for the information of the Bureau, the writer [name blacked out again] occupied Room 7 of the Shirley Courts, which is next to Room 8, which was occupied by William O. Lucas and his family. A technical surveillance of the room was instituted by the writer generally with negative results. Conversations which were overheard and which were discernable were not pertinent to this investigation.'[4]

Possibly the FBI were happy about the results of this surveillance, because the same report stated: 'Unless advised to the contrary by the Bureau, no surveillance of William O. Lucas and his wife and daughter will be conducted at Mexico City upon their return to Mexico City from Guatemala City.'

It would seem that Lucas had been absolutely forthcoming about himself and his earlier years in the USA, not only in his statements to the authorities, but to newspapers and periodicals for whom he sought to write. Again and again, judging from the blacked-out lines in the texts of these reports, it seems clear that someone in London was urging checks on Lucas. Most of these were SIS personnel, whose names have not been revealed, but one name in MI 5 occasionally missed the blacking-out, that of Guy Liddell, who seems to have wanted Lucas out of any links with American Intelligence at all costs.

Presumably this worried the FBI a great deal, as their investigation of Lucas shows. His every movement during travels from the USA to Mexico and various territories in Latin America were monitored in astonishing detail. The following reports will show the almost ridiculous diligence with which such surveillance was carried out:

1. 'Source D ascertained that William O. Lucas, his wife and daughter arrived at Ixmiquilpan, Hidalgo, in a two-door blue Packard Clipper Sedan bearing New York license plates 7K952 at 5.30 pm on 17 February 1944.... Lucas stopped for gas at the Dodd Service Station at Ixmiquilpan and thereafter proceeded to Mexico City. Although the drive from Ixmiquilpan to Mexico City should normally take approximately two hour's driving time, Lucas did not arrive in Mexico City until shortly after 1 am 18 February, due to tyre trouble.'

2. Also on 18 February: 'Lucas attempted to obtain room facilities at the Shirley Courts in Mexico City. Inasmuch as the Shirley Courts were totally occupied, and.... as he had made no previous reservation request, Lucas was unable to find a room at the Shirley Courts and did finally find a room at the Royal Courts in Colonia del Valle.'

3. 'At 7 pm --------- [blacked out] came to Lucas's room....

where they were received by Lucas and his family. They greeted each other in English and sounded as though they were old friends.'

4. 20 February, 1944: 'It was observed by Source D that Lucas and his family had no visitors in their room on the premises of the Shirley Courts from 5 pm through the evening.'

5. 22 February, 1944: 'It was ascertained from Source F that Lucas, his wife and his daughter were issued war CC Priorities Numbers P-418, P-419 and P-420 for travel on Pan American Airways. It was ascertained from ------ that Lucas and his wife were living at the Shirley Courts around December 1942, at which time he was travelling around Mexico as a tourist. He last stayed at the Shirley Courts in Mexico City from 9 November 1943, to 14 November 1943, at which time he was believed to have departed from Acapulco.'

6. 3 March 1944: 'Lucas, his wife and daughter in the company of ------- made a tour of the properties of ----------- and several construction projects which are being made by ------ -, all of which are located within the properties. At 10.55 Lucas, accompanied by his wife and daughter, left and proceeded to Quezaltenango, Guatemala. This trip was made in the rented automobile in which subject and his family had arrived at Cantel ...... At 12.15 the group entered a grocery store, La Selecta, remaining in the place twenty five minutes.... During the entire afternoon and evening of 3 March 1944, subsequent to the return from the above described trip to Quezaltenango, Lucas and his family remained indoors and received no visitors.'

The reports continue, showing that surveillance was maintained, but recording the most boring details of the Lucas's everyday life; nothing was missed, but equally nothing of any vital importance was revealed. There were also reports such as this one from the Guatemala City Office: 'Will report the movements and contacts of Lucas ------- and those of his wife and daughter, and will continue the surveillance until they leave the Republic of Guatemala.' And yet another which stated 'Will make discreet inquiries in an effort to ascertain why Lucas has been surveilled by agents of President Ubico, and advise the Bureau by cable of the results.'[5]

One simple reason for all this may be that the American authorities were still baffled by the information Lucas produced from his freelance intelligence network, and by his ability to obtain almost as much on the Soviet Union as on Nazi Germany.

But that is only part of it: the truth is that Lucas had a number of enemies, at least some of them tucked away in Intelligence departments in London.

Whatever else they did or didn't achieve, these official records clearly indicate that Lucas existed and was not a fiction created by Wythe Williams.

THOSE MYSTERIOUS EARLY YEARS

The facts given to the United States authorities regarding Lucas's application for naturalization papers seem categorical enough. It is hard to believe that he would ever have risked giving false information on so vital a matter. Yet when one comes to check the information he gives on his parentage, there is almost nothing.

Mr Kyril Zinovieff, a distinguished authority on pre-World War I Russia, stated that, 'I know nothing about W.O. Lucas, or about his father, Otto Lucas. Nor am I able to find his name among conductors of the "Russian Imperial Opera Company". I have put the name of the Opera Company in inverted commas, since there was no such organization: the opera formed part of the Imperial Theatres. There was no one of the name of Lucas among the directors of the Imperial Theatres either.'[1]

Madame Nina Berberova of Princeton University, and another authority on pre-World War I Russia, also tells me that she 'has never heard or read the name of William Otto Lucas. There had never been a conductor of such name in the Imperial Opera.'[2]

Referring to the name of Caroline Yannutsch, of British nationality, described by Lucas himself as his mother, Madame Berberova added: 'I only know that a Russian (minor) woman-poet, Karolina Pavlova, born Janisch (1807-1893) existed, but it is not known if she had any children. In 1856 she left Russia for good and lived in Germany. She is completely forgotten now, and this lady was not of English extraction, but German.'[3]

Similarly I drew a blank with inquiries made of Count Tolstoi.

He had not heard of either the Lucas family or that of Luthen-heim (the family name of Lucas's wife). I was able to trace the directories of St Petersburg for the period 1900-1914, which contained alphabetical lists of residents including foreigners. This was the *Almanach de St Petersburg court, monde et ville.* Again there was no reference to Lucas or Luthenheim, though these directories included the names of all prominent personalities.

There was, however, one other reference book of the period which contained the names and addresses of all the residents of St Petersburg, a directory entitled *Ves' Petersburg,* dating from 1909 to 1912, which was in the Cyrillic alphabet. Here I had rather more success. In 1909 the name of William Otto Lucas was listed, at the address of 13 Torgovay. There was, however, no indication that he was in any way associated with the world of music. In the edition for 1912, under the same address, there was the name of "Wilhelm Lucas", and from the abbreviated description of his likely occupation it would seem that he was either studying or had completed studying a course of electrical engineering and construction work. This would tally with the kind of work Lucas took up after his courses at Riga University. On the other hand there is no indication that the William Otto Lucas, named as his father, was a musical conductor. The suggestion here, given entirely in abbreviated symbols, is that he might have been a landowner.

There is a clue to Lucas's wife's family. For the year 1912, in this same directory, there is an entry on Alexander Lutengeim of 24 Cposdeskya, St Petersburg. He is listed as a landowner.[4] Admittedly, there is a change in the spelling here, but the name is the only one which tallies, and the entry seems to be confirmed in the almanac. There is no indication of Lutengeim's profession, other than a vague hint that he might have been a medical practitioner.

So once again one comes up against the puzzle of who the family Lucas, or Van Narvig, really were. The story of a father who was a conductor of an orchestra in Imperial Russia appears to be without substance. Was this a deliberate alibi? Was Lucas's real name not Lucas, but something quite different?

In his own statement on his life Lucas claimed that, upon graduation from Riga University, he was in the employ of the General Electric Company and that he supervized construction of the street car system in Archangel (three lines and eleven miles) and Samara (five lines and 18 miles), as well as conducting a survey of water power resources in North Russia and the Upper Volga Basin for the Imperial Industrial Commission. During this period he also claimed that he contributed articles on engineering and rural electrification in *New Time* and *Industrial Gazette*.[5]

Lists at Riga University name a certain "Wilhelm" Lucas as having scientific proficiency certificates with a special certificate for electrical studies. The dates and age of the person in question tally with those for Lucas in this period. Nonetheless, this seems far from being the whole story, and it is likely that Lucas, whoever he was, conjured up all manner of cover stories for himself from quite an early stage in his life. There is the story in which he suggests he was first and foremost a Finn and served in the Finnish Army (for which there is no positive support). Then there is the information from Switzerland which names him as a secretive character known as "Werther"; while from Germany there emerges a whole series of pseudonyms. The real puzzle in all this is why, as now seems almost certain, Lucas should invent the story that his father was a conductor of the apparently non-existent "Imperial Opera Company"? This is so easily disproved that it seems pointless.

On the other hand, long experience of delving into the minds of spies shows that sometimes they find that the most outrageous claims will be accepted without question whereas much more modest alibis will be carefully scrutinized. I have myself had letters from no less than four people, two men and two women, who claim to have been personally recruited as spies at a very early age by Winston Churchill, not for any specific intelligence service but simply for the great man himself. Without being too critical or categoric, may I just say that all four are still alive and that their detailed evidence does at first glance suggest their claims are genuine. Yet, though their alleged fantastic escapades are often so outrageous or ludicrous as to be beyond belief, to disprove their cases is far from easy.

Limited details of an informant used by the British in the

early 1920's suggest another possible alias for Lucas. The code name was "Bill Findearth" (Finland?) and his name is mentioned in correspondence with friends of "Roger" in Switzerland. 'I am almost sure that "Bill Findearth" is "Werther",' states "Roger". 'I cannot prove anything, but the links are so close. As I understood it from others in the game, "Bill Findearth" was a contact of Professor A.C. Pigou, of King's College, Cambridge, and through his British mother there had been a link with the Pigou family. She had also had some links with British Naval Intelligence. Beyond that we, or rather I, knew very little. We were concerned solely with our network. I did inquire why this curious name of "Bill Findearth" was used for correspondence and I was simply told that "Werther" preferred it that way. Certainly I had the impression that he hoped that his friend Professor Pigou would put through such information to British Intelligence. But, suddenly, shortly after the outbreak of World War II, "Werther" seems to have become worried about the links to Pigou, because they abruptly dropped off. I am quite sure they did not go through any other channel.'

Born at Ryde, Isle of Wight, on 18 November 1877, Pigou was the son of Clarence George Scott Pigou, a retired Army officer from a family with Huguenot ancestry and associations with China and India. Young Pigou won a scholarship to Harrow where his father had also been educated and among his contemporaries were Winston Churchill, Leo Amery and George Trevelyan. At King's College, Cambridge Pigou read history under Oscar Browning, securing a first class in the history tripos in 1899. He distinguished himself as a debater in the Union and won the Chancellor's Medal for English verse. In 1902 he was elected to a King's Fellowship which he held for fifty seven years, unbroken by his brief period at London University. In his first book, *Principles and Methods of Industrial Peace*, published in 1905, he argued for a more equal distribution of income to increase economic welfare. He seems to have gone to surprising lengths to hide his support for revolutionaries and to avoid being linked to any political party. Yet he had a secret hankering after the life of a conspirator, and when the Russian Social Democrats, who had made London their headquarters in 1903, held their congress there in 1905, he attended. It was then that he took a decision to keep his new role a closely guarded secret, for a diary he kept that year was entirely in code and contained references solely to links with the Social Democratic Party of Russia.

Pigou's coded comments for 1905 suggest that he was already committed to giving the revolutionaries illegal aid, if necessary. In one he stated: 'Advised Tchaikovsky [this must have been Nikolas Tchaikovsky, a relative of the composer] on financial routes for payment of arms shipments to Riga;' another entry reads: 'Established communication with Piatnitsky via George Flemwell in Switzerland: this is a permanent link by Verlet in Geneva.'[6]

Arthur Pigou's cryptic references to making financial arrangements for payments for 'arms shipments to Riga' indicate that a few Britons were aiding the revolutionaries in obtaining arms supplies. Maxim Litvinov, who had early associations with Britain, was himself in charge of gun-running in 1903, and undoubtedly he must have developed a British network to assist in this. But it was the sprucely attired intellectual, Nikolas Tchaikovsky, who spoke perfect English, who was the recruiter of agents in Britain and key man in the subterranean arms traffic. He was a welcome visitor to many London drawing-rooms and salons and was doubtless able to weigh up potential recruits on these occasions. Samuel Hobson, a Quaker won over to the cause of Russian revolutionaries, tells us how he himself was lured into the illicit arms traffic by Tchaikovsky. 'In the late winter of 1904 Tchaikovsky came to see me. He had something on his mind, but was slow, even cautious, to open it. Gradually, I realized that he wanted me to co-operate in shipping arms into Russia. They had bought 6,000 Browning revolvers in Boston, USA, and the serious job was to get them shipped, first to England, where they must be packed in a special way, and thereafter to Riga.'[7]

Hobson did not reveal the full details of this complex transaction, or who else was involved in it. A sum of £3,000 in the form of a banker's draft was paid into his bank account — the classic Russian ruse of involving an agent from the start. From that point onwards Hobson became an export merchant, ostensibly engaged in hardware and the lard trade. The revolvers were then brought to Britain, apparently without any difficulty, and taken to a warehouse near the Thames at East Ham, where a few trusted docker agents re-packed them in barrels of lard. According to Hobson, customs officials in Baltic ports had an instrument for probing lard barrels to test the consistency of the fat, though it seems more likely that this was done to check that the shipment was indeed lard and not guns. Holes punched in the barrels in certain positions ensured that the probing instrument would by-pass the revolvers.

There is a suggestion in the list of Russian underground contacts in Pigou's diary that Stalin was known to revolutionaries in Britain even in 1905, for on one page is the name "Josef Georgi — Berne", and this was certainly the name by which Stalin was known to the Bolsheviks in London. Pigou's knowledge of Stalin from these distant revolutionary days may have made him singularly uncritical of the communist dictator, for in the late thirties and throughout the forties he went out of his way to praise Stalin's achievements.

Pigou's passion for mountaineering resulted in frequent trips to Switzerland. In World War I he solved his problem as a pacifist by volunteering for service in the Friends' Ambulance Unit. He remained at his post at King's in term time, but served in the FAU during vacations. *The Friend* of 25 December 1914, noted his departure with a group of five others to join the Unit in France. The list of members of the FAU 1914-19 includes him under Cambridgeshire as 'A.C. Pigou, served December, 1914 — to April, 1915.' F.R. and R.M. Leavis are also listed among the members, and Philip Noel-Baker, or Baker as he then was, took command of the Unit. At the end of June 1915, Noel-Baker and Pigou switched to the Red Cross Organization, possibly because another colleague, George Trevelyan, had taken a leading part in organizing a British Committee in Aid of Italian Wounded when Italy entered the war at the end of May 1915. A Red Cross Ambulance Unit was sent to work on the Italian Front and Noel-Baker and Pigou joined it, the latter presenting his car to the Unit. Red Cross records show that he served as a chauffeur from 18 December 1915 to 9 April 1916. Some mystery attaches to the reasons for Pigou's departure from the Red Cross service in April 1916. Official records provide no clue. George Trevelyan, when questioned once about Pigou's ability as a driver, replied that the professor was 'apt to pretend to be rather a worse driver than he really was. Never understood the reason why. But he never had as many accidents as suggested. I sometimes think his stories of accidents and delays were intended to cover up his forays into Switzerland during service on the Italian front.'

Forays into Switzerland? If Trevelyan knew the purpose of these, he was certainly not admitting anything. At this time Red Cross personnel were often recruited for the Secret Service, as they were well placed to pick up useful information. Somerset Maugham, for example, had joined a Red Cross Unit as an ambulance driver, dresser and interpreter in France in 1914 and shortly afterwards transferred to the Secret Service. Geoffrey Winthrop Young wrote of meetings and long talks between himself, Somerset Maugham and Pigou. Maugham spent a year as a secret agent in Geneva before being sent to Russia in 1917. That Pigou was acting as an unpaid intelligence agent and courier for a group of Russian revolutionaries between Switzerland and Britain in this period and possibly later seems probable. Whether he could have been working for both the Allies and the revolutionaries is possible, but doubtful. What is certain is that he was in touch with the Czech Intelligence organization and with members of the American Red Cross (both of which to some extent worked with British Intelligence) and also with the editor of a socialist newspaper, *DeIncke Listy*, in Cleveland, Ohio, who had contacts with British Intelligence and the Russian revolutionaries in Switzerland. The last-named included one Josef Martinek, who wrote to D. Petrovsky, one of the earliest Comintern agents in Britain, that, 'the cause of the exiles in both the USA and England was greatly aided in 1916 by the messages of encouragement from our friends in Switzerland and Italy and the brief, but free from all cumbrousness, intelligence reports carried to and from by our own OGiPU who served in the British Red Cross on the Italian — Austrian front on leave from his Cambridge college and used his own vehicle on our behalf.'[8]

This obviously refers to Pigou and is a clever playing around with letters. As to how and when Lucas himself might have come into contact with Pigou, either earlier — through his mother or much later in his career, is totally unclear. But why should he use the most unusual code-name of "Findearth"? I have not come across one instance of this name in any telephone directory. It is always possible that one of the reasons for such subterfuge was the need to protect members of his family, possibly especially on his mother's side, because so far no trace of this family has emerged.

Pigou's links with revolutionaries continued for many years. He was an unofficial adviser to Theodore Rothstein, who had become a propagandist for the Bolsheviks under the name of "John Bryan" and was a leading Soviet agent in Britain after the Russian Revolution. For a brief period towards the end of World War I Professor Pigou got himself work in Government service; a part-time appointment at the Board of Trade in 1918, for which he had little inclination, and it seems fairly certain that he took it up reluctantly in order to help the revolutionaries. But at no time did he show any open interest in the revolutionary movement.

'I cannot say just how early on in the 1920's "Findearth," or "Werther" had direct links with Professor Pigou,' states "Roger", 'but they certainly met on the Professor's various trips to Switzerland. They swapped information over quite a long period, and through Pigou "Werther" obtained details of the setting-up of the Soviet intelligence network in the USA in the years immediately after the Revolution. This network was intended to collaborate with the parallel network in Britain and the chief Soviet courier on the American-British route was Jacob Nosivitsky. By means of forged identification papers Nosivitsky operated under the names of James Norson and James Anderson, travelling from the Detroit Medical College, first as assistant surgeon in the *Mauretania*, then as ship's doctor in the *Melita*. In June 1919, when he arrived in Liverpool under one of his aliases, Nosivitsky was arrested and taken to Scotland Yard for questioning.'

While "Werther" certainly seems to have given some aid and a good deal of intelligence to anti-fascist organizations and even to some who were friendly towards the Soviet Union, it is clear that he was — again to quote "Roger" — 'anxious to have a foot in all camps and not least to pass on information about Soviet activities in building American networks to the American authorities. It may have been this which eventually caused a shut-down in his relations with Pigou. Certainly something went very cold there, and the "Findearth" link was cut out completely. I believe "Werther" thought he had been the object of a smear campaign from someone in London to the US authorities, probably the FBI.'

Professor Walter Kendall has stated that 'the extent to which a Comintern network existed already in 1920 has been under-rated.'[9] As far as Britain was concerned, this was undoubtedly true, though some of the counter-espionage agencies had a strong suspicion that there was something much more professional brewing behind the scenes than the amateurish pranks of people such as Sir Francis Meynell and Sylvia Pankhurst, whose blunderings into these deep waters made even the incompetent Mata Hari seem professional in comparison.

While one cannot be a hundred per cent sure that "Findearth", "Werther" and Lucas were one and the same person, or that Lucas was not building up alibis for himself into which he could escape in an emergency, there is a vital clue in London which throws a new light on the subject. A man with the code-name "Findearth" was one of the unofficial contacts used by Sir Basil Thomson when he organised the Special Branch at Scotland Yard after World War I and devoted his attention to combating the early menace of Soviet espionage and, more especially, subversion in Britain. His own papers, made available to this author when researching the life of David Lloyd George, specifically mention "Findearth": a lively and accurate informant on Soviet activities in Finland as they concern the United Kingdom.'

This, of course, points very much in the direction of the "van Narvig" Finnish contacts and, not least, to Lucas's own account of his life in Finland in the early 1920's. As will shortly be seen from independent evidence there is proof of yet another code-name for this mystery man, this time "Dmitri", who was supposed to be rescuing people from Soviet Russia, and also passing on intelligence on pro-Soviet Finns operating between Britain and America. It was the intelligence received from "Findearth" on these Finns which enabled Sir Basil

Thomson to score a number of successes. "Findearth" tipped him off that there was a secret Finnish courier operating for the USSR who had been instructed to come to London and who had already slipped through customs. This turned out to be Errki Veltheim, a Finnish Comintern representative, who was carrying cipher letters. Veltheim had linked up with a certain Lieutenant-Colonel Cecil John L'Estrange Malone, elected a Member of Parliament as a Coalitionist in the 1918 "Coupon Election", but who became a member of the executive of the Communist Party of Great Britain, and who actively plotted to establish an underground "Red Officers Corps" in Britain to pave the way for a communist takeover of the state. Veltheim was arrested as he left Colonel Malone's house at Chalk Farm, London. With him was a Miss Gilbertson, Sylvia Pankhurst's secretary, and when Veltheim was eventually released from detention, she went with him to Russia.

Colonel Malone was both flamboyant and fanatical in everything he tackled. In 1920 he created a sensation at a meeting at the Albert Hall by stating that he hoped the Russian revolution 'would soon be followed by a British revolution. What are a few Churchills and Curzons on the lamp-posts compared to the massacre of thousands of human beings?' Sentenced to six months' imprisonment on a charge of sedition, Malone left the Communist Party within eighteen months and joined the Labour Party, for whom he sat as MP for Northampton from 1928-31. An honest man, with an heroic war record, Malone was foolish enough to allow the disgust he felt at the corruption and chicanery of the Lloyd George administration to swing him to extremes. He was also fundamentally opposed to the idea of British intervention in Russia's civil war. In World War II his services were accepted in the Royal Navy from 1943-45.

Lucas was, according to both British and American sources, well informed on other Finnish and Scandinavian Soviet links in the network extending to Britain and the USA. This especially applied to Salme Murrik, an Estonian, who was sent to Britain by the Comintern to assist in setting up the Communist Party of Great Britain. Both Salme and her sister, Hella, had set up a "safe house" in Finland for couriers between Russia and other countries in Western Europe and

50

also the USA. Salme Murrik slipped into Britain illegally, without any papers, and in 1924 married Rajani Palme Dutt, an Indian at Oxford University.

One has the feeling that at this time Lucas had several problems to sort out all at once and that in some cases they conflicted with one another. Protection of his family rather than himself was his priority, and this may be the explanation not merely for the various names he used, but also for the fictitious characters he created as additional and baffling alibis. Having suffered heavy financial losses as a result of the Revolution, he had to carve out a new career for himself. At this stage he seemed to be torn between building up a business and crusading for a better world, a conflict which never left him. Meanwhile he found, sometimes to his cost, sometimes to his advantage, that he had friends on both sides in the Russian camp. This may have made him even more cautious in covering up his traces when involved in espionage, and such decisions as he had to take from time to time cannot have been easy, but on the whole he seems to have acted with common-sense and justice. It is this quality of his of never allowing problems to demoralize or upset him that marks him out as the super-spy

The task from now on is to try to sift out and analyze these alibis, and to try to ascertain whether some of them might after all be linked to other personalities. What the alibis, or code-names, contributed in the way of information was often just as important, in its own way, as that which Lucas himself supplied. Looking at the information so far it almost seems as though there could have been two "Superspies", Lucas and A.N. Other. If Lucas leaned towards supplying intelligence to the USA, then A.N. Other, "Findearth" or "Walter", appeared to want to pass information to the British.

6

BALLOONING OUT OF RUSSIA

Lucas merely states in his 'record of experience' that, having lost all his Russian properties in the Bolshevik Revolution, he 'entered general Korniloff's Volunteer Army as a divisional staff officer.'[1] He gives no date for this, but, if the statement is correct, then it must have been very early in the Civil War because, as we have seen, Korniloff himself was killed at the very beginning of that conflict. After that various anti-Bolsheviks took over the running of the volunteers, men such as Denikin, Yudenich and Wrangel.

He also claims he was taken prisoner by the Reds, spent five months and seventeen days in an Arctic prison camp, escaped 'four hours before my scheduled execution in January 1919, and reached the Finnish frontier in April, after a three months trek through the Arctic wasteland.'[2]

There may be excellent reasons for Lucas not telling the full story of his service with the anti-Bolsheviks, even to Wythe Williams, not least to protect colleagues and especially anyone who might have helped him to escape. It is even possible that he was shielding someone like Andrei Alexandrovich Zhdanov, who later became Secretary-General of the Soviet Communist Party, and whom he claimed to have rescued during the Russian Revolution. Zhdanov, according to Lucas, 'had been my best friend since, as a chubby little boy he shared the same bench with me in our school classroom. We were fellow officers in a crack regiment of Imperial Guards that was almost anni-hilated in 1914 at Tannenberg. When he joined the Reds after the Revolution and was captured, it was I who arranged for his escape.'[3]

Lucas did not tell this story until 1952, some four years after Zhdanov's death. It is probable that Lucas was sometimes put in an awkward position during the Russian Civil War when he came upon old friends who were now in the opposing camp. This happened to quite a few people at this time, raising problems which cut right across family loyalites as well as old friendships. At worst this resulted in the person who was placed in this unhappy position being trusted by neither side, and sometimes actually being liquidated.

This could explain why Lucas as a form of self-protection arranged a cleverly conceived number of aliases for himself, aiming to cover his tracks completely in certain countries of the world, if, indeed, not in all of them. While this was undoubtedly done for his own benefit, it also served to protect his friends and contacts, something which he achieved over more than a quarter of a century rather more successfully than most professional spies.

It may have been because he had, against all odds, so cleverly organized his own escape from a Soviet prison camp, that he decided to help others to escape during the years of the Civil War and right into the 1920's, regardless of which side they were on.

His story of Zhdanov having been in 'a regiment of Imperial Guards' is, however, somewhat puzzling, as this remarkable character, the son of a school inspector, was at the age of sixteen already the leading spirit of a Marxist group at Tver (now known as Kalinin), and after the Revolution he emerged as one of the most zealous and enthusiastic supporters of the Communist regime.

Reino Hatsonen, a Finn who had been caught with his wife inside Soviet Russia in the latter part of the Civil War, claimed to the author that he was rescued and brought back to Finland through the direct help of Lucas. 'I did not know him under that name,' said Mr Hatsonen, 'but I recognized him beyond all doubt when I saw his photograph in a book published in Helsinki in 1982.'[4]

Mr and Mrs Hatsonen were under house arrest on suspicion of being members of an underground Finnish movement opposed to the Soviet Union. 'We were, in fact, nothing of the sort,' stated Mr Hatsonen. 'We had only tried to find some relatives of my wife and suddenly found ourselves trapped inside Russia. One day a message was smuggled in to me from someone using the code-name of Dmitri. It was to warn me to be ready with our belongings at a certain hour of the night the following week. We were told to go to the cellar and wait there until someone arrived.

'This is all a long time ago now and the rescue went so swiftly and efficiently that I cannot recall all the details. A Finn called for us and, while a friend of his kept the house-watcher occupied, he led us away under a hedge and across a field. When we got there, to our astonishment, the man who called himself Dmitri and another man who spoke Finnish were inflating a balloon.'[5]

From Mr Hatsonen's letters, and his answers to a series of questions I put to him, I pieced together the story of what must have been one of the very first rescues of this nature, made by a home-made and extremely primitive balloon. I have not been able to pin-point the exact place from which the Hatsonens left the Soviet Union, as they themselves were not told where they had been taken by those who arrested them. But it would seem to be somewhere in the vicinity of Petrozavodsk which is slightly more than a hundred miles from the border with Finland. My own guess is that the exact site of their departure was probably less than fifty miles from the border.

The Hatsonens were alarmed when first told that their escape would be made by balloon, though of course they were hugely delighted at this chance to get away. "Dmitri" told them that he had piloted planes while serving in the Russian forces during World War I and that he had studied the art of balloon construction. It was a very dark night and the Hatsonens had very little chance to see what was happening, but they recalled that the balloon was fully inflated less than ten minutes after they reached it. They recalled that while they were waiting "Dmitri" said he had plans for using such a balloon in Finland in connection with timber hauling.

Beneath the balloon was a platform with rails around it. Huddled together in this were the Hatsonens, "Dmitri" and his assistant. A short while after the ascent, which to the passengers seemed painfully slow, they were all soaked by torrential rain. "Dmitri", who was in charge of the balloon, told the others to lie down on the platform while he frantically baled out the rain water. After a while the rain ceased and the balloon gained height, and increased speed. How long the journey to freedom took they could not remember, but they thought it must have been about an hour. If that was all then they were certainly much nearer the Finnish border than they imagined.

'We just missed a clump of trees when we came down with a bump,' said Mr Hatsonen, 'and we ploughed into some very low bushes. "Dmitri" ushered us away from the balloon while his friend guarded it. He assured us we were safely in Finland and accompanied us for about a mile to a farm-house. By this time it was getting quite light. I noticed that Dmitri carried a map and a compass as well as a torch. He told us to knock on the door of the farm-house, but that he had no time to waste and must go. Then he shook hands and wished us well.'

The Hatsonens never saw "Dmitri" again, but they heard later that a mysterious ex-Army officer who had connections in both Germany and Russia was engaged in rescuing people from the USSR and bringing them into Finland and Sweden. In a few cases this had been achieved by balloon.

In 1922 Lucas was making a valiant effort to recoup the losses he and his family had suffered in the Russian Revolution. He mobilised what financial resources he still had left in the United States and established import and export offices in Helsingfors, Reval, Copenhagen, Warsaw, Berlin and Vienna, with Chicago as headquarters of the organisation. He seems to have been dealing in automotive and electrical equipment, food stuff, textiles and — in his own words — 'anything that found a market'.

In between all this chasing around the world in quest of business he managed to find time to write a book, *Peace on Earth*, a novel based on pre-war Russia which was published in German by a firm in Stuttgart.

Then, suddenly, he seems to have changed his plans totally, whether purely for business reasons, or in the interests of rescue work one does not know. He purchased a large tract of forest in Finnish Karelia and contracted for the entire output with Swedish and British lumber firms. Because of the proximity of the tract of land to the zone of the then threatening war between Finland and Soviet Russia, the banks refused to co-operate, and Lucas had to strain the financial resources of his firm to finance the venture.

'Heading an army of three hundred Finnish lumberjacks,' he wrote, 'I entered this Karelian wilderness in the fall of 1922, spent the winter and the following spring and summer in supervising the felling, hauling and cutting of the timber and its shipment on fifty-two lake and canal steamers. In the meantime a trusted employee, who had attended to the sales and collections in Stockholm and London, decamped with the proceeds to the United States where, gambling the money away, he fell a victim to self-destruction. To satisfy the creditors, I had to strip myself of all personal and real property, which spelt the end of this phase of my career.'[6]

It was a disaster for Lucas, but, with his usual nonchalance and sense of realism, he merely commented that he 'started from the bottom once more.' The advice he gave himself was 'Go West, young man,' and he returned to the United States, becoming associated in early 1924 with Olin H. Landreth, a consulting engineer of Fifth Avenue, New York.

For the next two years Lucas worked on various engineering projects and translated books and engineering and sales literature for the principal New York translation bureaux. Then in May 1926, he joined the publicity staff of Paramount Production in New York and Hollywood. He was put in charge of foreign publicity and as a side line wrote a series of articles on motion picture production which were published in *Die Woche* (Berlin), *Illustrierte Zeitung* (Hamburg), *Woche in Bild* (Vienna), *La Filme* (Paris), *Allers Familje Journal* (Stockholm), *Veckans Kroenika* (Helsingfors) and in smaller publications in Prague, Warsaw, Riga, Belgrade and Bucharest.

At the same time he also wrote the story and continuity for the motion picture, *Where Satan Fails* and contributed to the continuity of *Kid Boots.* There was, however, somewhat of a mystery in late 1927 when Lucas resigned from Paramount because, so he said, 'of basic difference of opinion over the exploitation of Emil Jannings.'[7]

There is no doubt that Lucas was keeping up his contacts with intelligence services in Europe and Russia just as much as in the rest of the world. He was still hoping to establish some relationship with British Intelligence, but had been bitterly disappointed by their response to his approaches. 'I was regarded as a problem,' he told a friend during this period.

'They gave the impression that they thought I knew too much and, because of my background, I might be leading them up what the British called "the garden path".'

After he left Paramount he joined the firm of D.W. Sanger & Co., of New York and Chicago, as a senior sales executive. In 1929 he established an investment securities business of his own in New York, which continued until the end of 1930. And still he devoted himself to collecting intelligence from Europe as he already foresaw the threat of Germany being taken over by reactionary forces. In his own mind Germany and Russia posed almost equal threats to world peace. It was this that increasingly fostered his desire to be a one-man intelligence agent, giving warnings of what he foresaw to any who would listen to him; at that time, though, very few would, least of all in the Americas.

Then, late in 1930, he was approached by two former Wall Street associates, and he accepted their offer of becoming general manager of the Vine-Glo Corporation, the distributing outlet of the Californian Grape Growers Association, operating under the sponsorship of the Federal Farm Board. He successfully piloted this organization through the two worst depression years until a complete change of policy by the Federal Government, prior to the presidential election of 1932, necessitated a quick liquidation of the enterprise.

Up to then Lucas had always visualized himself as a successful *entrepreneur*, but a series of defeats in Finland and the USA had changed his mind. From then onwards he saw life somwhat differently: first, he wanted to succeed as a writer and reporter on current events, secondly, he wished to impress on the Western world his fears for the future.

He started in somewhat haphazard fashion, writing a few articles on economic affairs, some short stories, and a novel which was never to be published. At that time he was living in Brooklyn; he became an ardent fan of the Brooklyn Dodgers and wrote a number of stories about baseball. Yet despite his experiences and his fluency in several languages (he wrote and spoke five principal languages with ease and also read words in nine additional languages), he found it almost impossible to become the prophetic and eagerly read political writer he desired to be. Even at the end of 1935 there was still a reluctance in many circles in the USA to pay serious attention to what was happening in Europe.

Next he tried to interest some people in Western Intelligence circles in what he had to say. A major stumbling block was that the United States at that time had no proper secret service, merely branches of naval and military intelligence. Another obstacle was the strong tendency in all parties and groups towards isolationism and what some called 'minding our own business'. It may have been foolish but it was understandable: Americans felt they had been dragged into a futile First World War which had been started by other peoples and had solved nothing, and could not yet see that what was happening in Europe, the Middle East and the Far East was ultimately very much 'own business'.

It was about this time that Lucas made various trips to Europe, specifically to Germany, Scandinavia, Switzerland and Britain. He picked up some useful intelligence and began to build a small network of informants. Essentially he was a freelance spy, knowing what kind of a world he would like to see develop, and willing to help any secret service in the Western world who would listen to him, notably Britain and Finland to begin with. He had contacts with magazines in Paris, Stockholm, Prague, Budapest, Vienna, Warsaw and Bucharest and all of these proved useful in enabling him to build his own library of clippings. As he was constantly moving around he had to conduct an extensive correspondence around the world, while at the same time he set out to teach himself about radio communications. As a result of this he built not merely one transmitting and receiving set, but three or four before he found the right answer. As an amateur radio ham he was probably well ahead of most others in those days. (His requests for information went out in a clever code which he worked into his articles — which were mainly about show-business and films — posting them to friends so as not to arouse suspicion in areas where they could easily be compromised.)

Because of his mother's British background (something he always stressed), it was thought by some of his friends that he might apply for British rather than American citizenship. The truth was, however, that he found far less scope for individual enterprise in Britain than in the USA. 'In America they welcome ambition and effort,' he once said, 'but in Britain they seem to resent it, or envy it. I hope one day that attitude will change. It is a sad sign in many ways as it reflects the gradual decline of that once great nation.' Lucas also hoped to establish some rapport with Britain's Secret Intelligence Service, especially on Germany even before the advent of Hitler. 'Nobody seemed to be interested, except for one or two people in Naval Intelligence. I suspect some either thought I knew too much (in the espionage world this is sometimes even more of a liability than knowing too little), or just mistrusted a foreigner. What was unforgiveable much later was that at least one person in the British Security set-up tried to smear my name by passing unfavourable reports on me to the USA.' This information was contained in a letter written about a year before war broke out to a British friend who had close connections with the British Naval Intelligence Division.

However, those tense and often worrying years between the wars had not been all frustration for Lucas. He seems to have settled down happily in America after becoming a naturalized US citizen in 1930. Shortly after this, when applying for a post, he stated: 'I have travelled three times around the world, have visited every country in the northern hemisphere. I have written numerous baseball stories which, if anything, proves my one hundred per cent Americanization.'[8]

Curiously his wife (the former Margared Luthenheim) does not seem to have become a naturalized American citizen until 1943. Indeed, her first passport, upon which was also written the name of her daughter, was not issued until 9 February 1944, in Washington.

In 1934 Lucas received an invitation from his old friend, Zhdanov, to visit him in Russia. Zhdanov was certainly taking a risk, but as he shared some of Stalin's doubts about the reliability of Comintern agents overseas, he probably thought Lucas could be used to give advice and, more importantly, to help direct propaganda against Nazi Germany. Again, it was not until after Zhdanov's death that Lucas told this story. 'You have wondered — like other Americans — what actually does go on in the mystery-enshrouded Kremlin and how the policies were evolved which now threaten the world,' he wrote in 1952.

'As it happens I am in a unique position to throw some light on these matters. I was the house guest many times of the second highest man in the Politburo. I rode with him, often in his armoured car, to the Kremlin.'[9]

Zhdanov had come from relative obscurity to a high position in the state by this time. Now in his forties, thick-set, dark-haired and with a black, military-style moustache, he was clearly somewhat of an authoritarian figure. At the fifteenth Communist Party Congress in 1925 he had been elected to the Central Committee for the entire Soviet Union. Then in 1934 he became Secretary of the Central Committee, directly under Stalin himself. He was a curious mixture of ruthless dictator and occasional liberal, sometimes devoted to purges within the Party, at others advocating a greater measure of democracy within that Party, urging that the social background of candidates for Party membership should not be considered. 'Whether a man's father was a capitalist or a worker should not matter,' he said.

What Lucas did not reveal was exactly how he received the invitation from Zhdanov, or how he had kept in touch with him over all these years. All he said 'after I came to the United States and became an American citizen, we still corresponded.' Did Zhdanov hope to persuade his old friend to become a Soviet agent in America, or at least an informant on news in general, or was this one of those surprising and dangerous friendships which somehow managed to be accepted in the era of Stalinist mistrust of all and sundry?

But there was another reason why Zhdanov was anxious to contact Lucas and that was the latter's Finnish connections. Zhdanov was well known as an expert on Finnish affairs in the Kremlin, and he would presumably have been well aware of Lucas's own contacts in that part of the world as well as being anxious to know just how the Finnish connection had been detected by Scotland Yard.

Lucas records that his old friend 'greeted me like a brother when I arrived at Leningrad and took me to his home. His children saluted me as their "American uncle".'[10]

The day after Lucas arrived in Leningrad Zhdanov took him to his office and introduced him to his chief, 'Sergei Kirov, who was not only the director of the Leningrad district, but a close colleague of Stalin. Lucas found Kirov to be 'a decent sort of fellow, not like the general run of bumptious Bolshevik leaders. At the time he was urging the enactment of liberal reforms and believed that Stalin would accept.'[11]

That was a first impression, and it may well have been correct. But later Lucas recorded how one day, when he was with Zhdanov in his office, a shot rang out. He and Zhdanov rushed out into the corridor and stumbled over a body. It was Kirov. His assassin, a young man named Nikolayev, was captured, though Lucas made no reference to what happened to him. It was at this very moment that Zhdanov took command and posted troops at strategic positions all around Leningrad in case the killing of Kirov might have been a signal for revolt. Almost immediately Stalin and Marshal Voroshilov came to Leningrad from Moscow by special train.

Meanwhile Zhdanov ordered Lucas to return to his apartment, adding that it would be unwise for him to be mixed up in this kind of a situation. This Lucas did and he sensed that Zhdanov's family were equally worried as to what might happen. Then, five days later, Zhdanov returned home in jubilant mood, saying that he had been praised by Stalin and appointed to succeed Kirov as director of Leningrad.

Over a bottle of Kakattin wine Zhdanov talked freely to Lucas. He revealed that Stalin had personally conducted the questioning of Kirov's murderer and had uncovered a plot by malcontent party members to overthrow the Politburo. It was because of this that Stalin had turned to Zhdanov for advice. Zhdanov had submitted a detailed paper on what needed to be done in future. A copy of this paper was passed to Lucas while he and Zhdanov were drinking. Lucas copied down some of the passages, including the following:

'The question of the very existence of the Soviet State is also the question of complete disassociation from foreign influences. One cannot go without the other. Disassociation of action as well as ideas, for ideas lead to actions. The opposition is pervaded with foreign ideas. Those ideas find expression in wrecking and sabotage of the Five Year Plan, in conspiracy and assassination. You do not destroy vipers unless you destroy their nests. You will never rid yourself of destructive foreign ideas unless you rid yourself of the opposition that feeds on those ideas. When the fate of the Soviet Union is at stake, you must not hesitate. You must impose your will.

'To impose your will you must be strong. To be strong you must command unquestioning obedience. To command that obedience you must maintain iron discipline. To maintain iron discipline, you must be held in fear. To be held in fear, you must inspire terror. At all times you must be the Supreme Leader, towering above all others. If there is a God, you must be above him. You must be the law, the power and the glory.'[12]

Lucas was appalled at what he read and handed the document back to Zhdanov with a look of disapproval. There was a long silence which was only broken by Zhdanov shouting, 'Say something! Call me what you like, but say something!'

It was clear to Lucas that his friend had suddenly taken an irrevocable step in the direction of tyrannous rule, but that at the same time his conscience and instincts told him this was wrong. Lucas replied that the whole proposal was nothing but blasphemy. 'If you believe there is no God, there can be no blasphemy,' was Zhdanov's response. The new ruler of Leningrad then poured out a diatribe about Britain and France conspiring against the Soviet Union and subsidizing Hitler. Yet, as Lucas commented at the end of it, 'we cannot agree, but, oddly, we can still remain friends.'

After he returned to New York Lucas learned of the latest purges in the USSR, the elaborately staged political trials and the cramming of millions of people into slave-labour camps. It was the signal that Stalin had accepted Zhdanov's programme, converting Lenin's party state into an authoritarian tyranny. By this time Zhdanov was a major member of the Politburo and President of the Foreign Affairs Committee of the Soviet Union, and in 1938 he became head of the Propaganda and Agitation Department of the Party.

7

FROM LENINGRAD TO BERCHTESGADEN

In April 1936 Lucas, in his capacity of chairman of the American Writers' Association, made allegations that communist activities were widespread in the offices of the US Works Progress Administration, especially in their guide-book project. This project had been reorganized only two months earlier after Lucas and Sam McCoy, former assistant director, had exposed what they called 'the Red influence' in the WPA.

Bearing out Lucas's charges, the New York *American* of 29 April reported that 'on Thursday night at 26 West 18th Street, New York, more than 360 members of the project will meet to vote to participate in the May Day united front parade of Communists and Socialists.' At the same time Lucas made public a copy of a letter sent to William L. Nunn, co-ordinating director of Federal projects, citing twelve examples, with names and dates, of alleged communist activities. Lucas's letter continued: 'But our Red friends' vituperous utterances against members of our organization have reached the boiling point. In connivance with Communist project executives they have stooped to frame-ups to cause discharge of members of our organization without due cause.'

The row over the Works Progress Administration was waged for the best part of two years. Lucas was joined by Ralph M. Easley, chairman of the executive council of the National Civic Federation, in attacking the WPA, who also complained of irregularities in an open letter to President Roosevelt. Lucas, himself a former WPA employee, who had resigned to take a post as publicity agent with the National Civic Federation, was accused of being an alien and was asked to provide proof of

63

American citizenship. It was pointed out that only such citizens could be employed by the WPA. Forthwith Lucas appeared at the WPA office to register his naturalization certificate in front of two witnesses.

It seems remarkably strange that Lucas should risk such publicity as this, but then he always was a crusader. One assumes that somehow, perhaps by a use of various aliases, he managed to keep his friends in the Soviet Union in the dark about his open condemnation of communist activities. It was about this time that he claimed to some people that he was partly responsible for the defection of General Walter Krivitsky from the service of the USSR. Krivitsky was without doubt the most important of all the early defectors from the Soviet Union and he was well known by Lucas. On the evening of 22 May 1937, Krivitsky returned from Moscow to his post as chief of the Soviet Military Intelligence (GRU) in The Hague. He had served the Russians for nearly twenty years and was depressed by what he had just heard of the fate of some of his best friends during Stalin's purges. 'I had worked sometimes sixteen and eighteen hours a day in the cause of Soviet communism,' he told Lucas, 'and I was very poorly paid. Even in my kind of top job by 1935 I did not earn enough to heat my Moscow apartment properly.'

Lucas urged Krivitsky to break with Stalin and 'tell the truth about him', because both men were convinced that Stalin was already planning to extend the hand of secret friendship to Hitler. There seems to be little doubt that it was Lucas who suggested that Krivitsky should defect to the USA rather than to Britain. 'We both knew that Britain had been penetrated by Russian agents in all spheres and that Krivitsky would be in danger if he talked too freely to the British,' said Lucas. 'I warned Krivitsky that if the British had any information as to his movements in the United States or Canada, he would find this passed on to the USSR and he would be relentlessly tracked down.'

Krivitsky told of a talk with Kedrov, one of the prosecutors in the purge trials of 1937, on forced confessions. Kedrov told Krivitsky: 'You don't know what can be made of a human being when you have him in your hands. We've had dealings here with all kinds, even with the most dauntless of men, and nevertheless we broke them down and made what we wanted of them.'[1]

Eventually Krivitsky defected in Paris, went to Hyères and took a passport in the name of Edward Miller, an Austrian engineer, to escape to the Western world. Lucas warned Krivitsky to take special care wherever he was either in the USA or Canada and that for some years to come he would have to keep on the move because the Russians would track him down. According to the late Isaac Don Levine, a noted historian, Krivitsky revealed that 'at least two fully fledged Soviet spies were in the inner sanctums of the British government [sic]. One of them was a code clerk in the secretariat of the Cabinet. Krivitsky knew only the last name, King. The other was on the inside of the Council of Imperial Defence. Krivitsky could describe his appearance, he knew something of his background, but did not know his name.' This information was contained in Levine's book, *Eye Witness to History* (1954). Later Levine himself told the author that 'a writer using the pseudonym William van Narvig informed me that he had warned Krivitsky that someone inside the British Establishment was passing on to the Russians details of his movements, and that it looked as though the source was in Britain's Embassy in Washington or that in Paris.' This could have pointed in the direction of the late Sir Anthony Rumbold in Washington or Donald Maclean in Paris.

Admittedly this statement, allegedly by Lucas, came at a time when it was already believed that Krivitsky had been betrayed by a British diplomat and Donald Maclean, who had served in Paris at that particular time, was a suspect. But it was not until years later that suspicion pointed to Sir Anthony Rumbold, a close friend of Donald Maclean (who had been best man at his wedding), who had been in the British Embassy in Washington at this period.

That Krivitsky was in fact tracked down by the Russians is abundantly clear. Mrs Beryl Edwards of Badgers Hall, Scissett, in Yorkshire told me on 18 June 1981 that when she was nine years old she went to Canada where she lived with her mother. When World War II broke out she was employed as a driver for the British–Canadian Inspection Board (inspection of munitions factories). While doing this work she was asked by one Gordon Cowan, of the Telecommunications set-up in Montreal, to put up Krivitsky, his wife and small son at her home and to drive him around. Together they went to Montreal and sometimes other places. They were usually followed by a RCMP (Royal Canadian Military Police) car for protection and RCMP members came to her home to interview Krivitsky on occasions. Krivitsky's cover name in Montreal was "Walter Thomas". She never saw exactly where he went; she would drop him at a certain point and he would then make his way on foot to his rendezvous. According to Mrs Edwards, he was always afraid of being discovered by the NKVD (the predecessors of today's KGB). On one occasion they were followed by a strange car (not from the RCMP) and she had to turn into an alley, drive into a garage, switch off the lights and stay there until it had gone past.

Krivitsky was actually detected by the Russians in Montreal, and once he suspected they had tried to break into Mrs Edwards' home. He found that some papers, which he had left under his bed had been burnt. He questioned his son who was not responsible. It was then that he warned his wife: 'If I am ever found dead and they tell you I committed suicide, don't believe them. I shall never kill myself, but the NKVD will make my death look like suicide.' This was, of course, exactly what happened when Krivitsky was found shot dead in a hotel room in Washington in February 1941. Washington police declared that an investigation had convinced them he had taken his own life.[2]

Prior to this Krivitsky had made various trips to Britain. Each time he returned he complained to Mrs Edwards: 'They won't listen to me.' His experience in many ways was similar to that of Lucas.

It was because of the high regard and trust he had for Wythe Williams, both as man and as a journalist, that Lucas decided to pin upon him almost all his hopes of making people heed his warnings about the future and war in Europe. He had studied Williams' modest suburban newspaper, *Greenwich Time*, and decided that, providing this well-informed and perceptive editor would give him enough space, much could be achieved. 'Give me the space,' he told Williams, 'and I'll give you scoop after scoop. Wait and see: in time people will sit up and take notice. What is more you can publicize my views and news and your paper by building yourself up as a radio commentator.'

In his daily newspaper Williams had been concentrating for some time on getting exclusive stories from Europe. It was this which had impressed Lucas. Most of the stories came through connections Williams had established during his many years as a foreign correspondent, but he also secured a few scoops from European refugees. One, which had been copied by other papers and journals all around the world, was that of the horse-whipping of Dr Josef Goebbels by the husband of a woman with whom the German Propaganda Minister had been having an affair.

'That single story has been repeated in countless papers and in different languages,' said Lucas. 'It just shows what can be achieved. But I'll do much better than that for you.'

Lucas's strength was that his contacts in Communist Russia were just as good as his contacts in Nazi Germany. It was at this point that he explained that a friend high up in Soviet circles made it possible for him to travel to all parts of the Soviet Union, even to Siberia on occasions and the Crimea and Central Russia as well.

'When did you last make such a trip?' inquired Williams.

'Well, I've only just got back to the USA after a ten-thousand mile journey through Russia and Siberia.'

'Good God! But why should this pal of yours give you such help? Travel in the Soviet Union is pretty well restricted, isn't it?'

'I helped him escape liquidation in the revolution. That's why he feels he owes me a favour or two.'

Lucas then casually mentioned that on the way back from Russia 'I stopped off at Berchtesgaden.' Naturally Williams was astonished and asked for more details. Though Lucas would not give much away he said that he had developed close ties in German ruling circles from the time he visited a relative who was one of Hitler's closest aides during the abortive Munich putsch in 1923. He explained that when, much later, Hitler came to power this relative was given a post on Hitler's staff at his mountain retreat, the Berghof, in the Bavarian Alps.

'I stayed with my relative for some weeks and I kept my ears open. You can take it from me that the second world war is now imminent. Very soon I shall be able to give you an exact date.'

Lucas backed up his promises of a series of sensational scoops by providing Williams with analytical notes on his recent travels in Russia and Germany. Williams admired not only his talent for getting such information, but his skill in summarizing it and drawing conclusions from it. There was also the fact that a service such as Lucas promised to provide would cost far less than setting up a private foreign news service, which *Greenwich Time* certainly could not afford.

'There's only one problem,' said Williams. 'Much of your material is so highly sensational that it just can't be used — at least not yet — by a newspaper in a neutral country.'

'They all say that,' replied Lucas, 'but I didn't expect you to take that line. Neutral you may be for a while, but sooner or later the United States will have to join the fray. In any case, once war comes, you'll have to report it.'

What finally impressed Williams, and persuaded him to take risks in printing and publicising Lucas's more sensational stories was the man's crusading zeal. Williams had seen one world war at first-hand as a correspondent in France in the 1914–18 era, and he shared much of Lucas' thinking on the need for Americans to keep themselves well informed and thus be prepared to face up to a dreadful future. His realization that total isolationism was something which the United States could not sustain much longer was probably brought about by Lucas's warning that Hitler would undoubtedly be joined by Japan in a global war which would aim directly at America.

'One final question,' said Williams. 'What about Russia? Surely she is on the side of the Allies?'

'Don't you believe it. Stalin is out to extend and build his own empire inside Eastern Europe. Have no doubt about that. His idea will be to move across Europe at the right moment for him. He'll keep out of the war as long as possible, and if he does appear to join the Allies, it will only be to further his own aims, to batten on to the West for supplies and exploit the Allies in every way.'

These conversations are re-constructed partly from what

Wythe Williams himself has said and written and partly from the recollections of others who knew Wythe and had heard him talk about van Narvig. Before he went off on his travels again Lucas promised to fix up at least one or two vital informants inside the hierarchy of the Reich, not just at Berchtesgaden, but also at Karin Hall, Marshal Goering's private estate. Meanwhile Williams sought his own contacts who might use him from time to time as a radio commentator on foreign affairs.

As to what happened next, Williams' story differs totally from that which Lucas later told other people. No doubt the *Greenwich Time* editor felt a certain amount of disinformation was now essential to provide cover for his informant. Ten days later in that summer of 1939 Williams said he had a cablegram from Hamburg from Lucas which stated: 'Decided to go to Moscow. Reason later.' 'I admit that at this point my confidence in van Narvig was shaken,' wrote Lucas. 'But two weeks later, on 24 August, came the official announcement that Hitler and Stalin had signed their pact of non-aggression, friendship and mutual consultation. I understood then what must have taken my partner to Russia.'[3]

One can be sure that whatever method Lucas used to communicate with *Greenwich Time* on that occasion it was most certainly not a cable from Hamburg, which would have been an open invitation for the Gestapo to call on him for a chat. Also Lucas must have sent Williams a far fuller report than those two brief sentences. He must also have given an indication of the date when World War II would start The proof of this came when Williams was asked suddenly to appear on the Hobby — Lobby radio programme because one of their guest commentators had not turned up. Lowell Thomas the author, himself no mean authority on European affairs, was acting as master of ceremonies and, reminding Wythe that he had continually been predicting imminent war in Europe in his newspaper, he asked: 'If war is coming, when will it break out?'

'I believe another war will start during the first week of September,' replied Wythe without any hesitation.[4]

On 1 September 1939, in the early hours of the morning German armoured forces crossed into Poland.

To his credit Lucas also warned his friends in Britain that war would come within the next month. He did this by two methods, via an indirect approach to a member of Britain's SIS, and via British contacts with the PAKBO organisation in Switzerland. The message was terse: 'War not later than 2 September, according to present German plans. It will be a massive move into Poland and leave no doubt as to intentions: the aim is to finish off Poland within a week or two. But the real bomb is to come — a Nazi–Soviet Pact.[5] Williams' later account of events suggests Lucas went to Hamburg, met up with a Nazi whom he had known at Berchtesgaden, and posed as a committed Nazi supporter. He was told that Stalin had never taken seriously the British and French military missions which were even then in Moscow, that he was not preparing to make a deal with Hitler, and that within a week von Ribbentrop (then the Reich Foreign Minister) would probably fly to Moscow to sign an alliance between Germany and Russia.

It was this information which caused Lucas to decide to go to Russia. If possible, he wanted to get there before Ribbentrop arrived, so he went from Germany to Helsinki and asked for an early flight to Moscow. But the Russian consul in Helsinki was not helpful, saying that before he could provide a visa he would need to consult Moscow. Lucas got over this difficulty by asking the consul to consult his friend, Andrei Zhdanov, one of the most influential people in the Kremlin and tipped by many as Stalin's successor. 'Except for him,' said Lucas some years later, 'I never could have set foot there [in the USSR].'[6] He got a visa at once.

On this occasion Lucas was met by an aide and kept more or less incommunicado in the closely guarded Zhdanov villa while Zhdanov went to Moscow to witness the signing of the Soviet–German Pact. On his return Zhdanov told Lucas that the Kremlin had indisputable proof — stolen from the British Foreign Office — that Britain had demanded that Germany should turn eastwards against Russia as part of a secret deal to permit German rearmament. He seemed to suggest that Russia had her own agents inside the Foreign Office and mentioned a Dutchman who was implicated in an anti-Russian plot with the connivance of the Foreign Office and someone close to the Duke of Windsor. Lucas very much doubted some of this information and suspected the intention was that he should use it to make mischief between America and Britain. Equally, Lucas was alarmed by the fact that untold harm could be done because inside British Establishment circles, both in the Foreign Office and Intelligence, there were both pro-German and pro-Soviet supporters.[7]

One can only speculate as to whether Zhdanov might have guessed or suspected that Lucas passed information to American sources. If so, he obviously tried to take full advantage of this. But clearly, although the two men differed violently on political ideology, they shared a passionate hatred of Nazism and the menace of Hitler.

Zhdanov took Lucas along personally to the Institute of Political Action in Gorki Street, Moscow, a small, unimpressive building which, with its armed guards and barred doors, might easily have been mistaken for a prison. Lucas described the Institute thus: 'It is really the School for Traitors. It is the finishing school for perpetrators of treason over the entire world. Its students, all carefully selected foreigners, are doing post-graduate work. All absorb their fundamentals elsewhere and are picked for advance work in the fine art of preparing their homelands for revolution by setting old-line political parties against each other, fomenting racial and economic strife and pushing their countries into bloodshed and bankruptcy. I was admitted to the Institute as a visitor on the second day after the Hitler — Stalin Pact, which lit the match for World War II, was signed in 1939.[8]

On that occasion Zhdanov had to go personally to the Institute to explain how it was that the Politburo, which had always declared the Nazis as their chief foe and a force which must be expunged from the earth, had suddenly clasped hands with Hitler, the devil incarnate. It was left to Zhdanov to tell the foreign comrades the reasons for this about-turn in policies. It was on this occasion that Lucas met for the first time such future leaders of the communist world as Walter Ulbricht, who became Deputy President of East Germany as Stalin's nominee; Wilhelm Pieck, later President of East Germany; Li Li-San, a Chinese Communist who founded a school for Communist agents in Asia and afterwards became Stalin's deputy in Manchuria; and, finally, a handsome, grinning man who slapped Lucas on the back. 'When I last met him,' said Lucas, 'he was Commissar Antonio of the International Brigade in Spain, the brightest star of all Institute graduates and eventually set up communism of his own in Yugoslavia and broke relations with Stalin. His real name is Josip Broz: the world knows him as Marshal Tito.'[9]

In company such as this Lucas could hardly fail to pick up invaluable intelligence. Ulbricht he had known from student days when Lucas spent his holidays with an uncle near Leipzig, but the person who most interested him on that occasion was one he had known as Krasnodebski, a former second lieutenant in Lucas's regiment in the Imperial Guards. They had fought together at Tannenburg.

'The name is now Rutkowski,' whispered Krasnodebski.

'What are you doing here?' inquired Lucas.

'I saw you arrive with Zhdanov,' was the reply, 'so you undoubtedly know that I am organizing police bodies for the purging of eastern Poland.'

Then, with a glint in his eye, he strutted away, obviously proud of the new task assigned to him. Later this same man compiled a list of thousands of the names of Polish loyalists, followed the Red Army into Poland and eliminated most of them. He was alleged to have instigated the infamous Katyn Forest massacre as a result of which four thousand Polish officers were found in a mass grave. His reward was to be appointed President of Soviet Poland by Stalin under the name of Bierut, derived from the first two syllables of his last two aliases — Bierkowski and Rutkowski.

Andrei Zhdanov on that occasion, with the help of his interpreter, Alyosha, spelt out for the largely foreign audience what the Nazi–Soviet Pact meant. 'A new world war is soon to begin,' he stated exultantly, 'and it involves the capitalist powers, Germany on the one hand, France and England on the other.' Then he went on to explain how Communists had no concern in such a war, but they must conserve their strength while their opponents tore at each other's throats. Already France and England had tried to drag Russia into their evil plot, but Stalin had seen that this was a trap and had come to the conclusion that the wisest method of keeping Russia out of war was to have a non-aggression treaty with Germany. At the same time Zhdanov made it clear that this did not mean that Stalin approved of Hitler. When the two combatants eventually collapsed, as they surely would, then Stalin would give the signal for Russia to act.

Tito on that occasion showed Lucas a volume which contained a complete list of the Institute's instructors for a number of years. In that list were several American names, one of which was that of Eugene Dennis, later to become general secretary of the American Communist Party, subsequently convicted and jailed for criminal activities against the United States.

In his search for American names in this volume Lucas was interrupted by Aloysha, the interpreter who had been given instructions to take him back to Zhdanov's apartment. Though he was Zhdanov's guest he was not allowed any freedom of movement on his own. During their journey back to the apartment Lucas asked Aloysha who was the Kremlin's key representative in the United States. Aloysha laughed and shook his head: 'We don't entirely trust American Communists and you are not even a Communist. But I can tell you this: our head man is now in Mexico awaiting to be given permission to enter the USA.'

Before Lucas left Moscow he managed to find out the name of that man. It was none other than Gerhart Eisler, the German who long afterwards was to jump bail and escape from America on a Polish ship while awaiting trial in New York. But at that time, 1939, he was still trying to get into the USA. Cordell Hull, the US Secretary of State, had been adamant in refusing him entrance from Mexico because of his record of communist membership.

Later Cordell Hull was overruled when Eisler, the Soviet Union's key secret agent for the USA, was admitted on the special recommendation of none other than Mrs Eleanor Roosevelt, the wife of the President.

Andrei Zhdanov began to become a little suspicious of Lucas's motives in wanting to come to Moscow, especially when the latter told him that he hoped to be there when Ribbentrop arrived. How did he know this, asked Zhdanov, as only about fifty people in the whole of Russia knew? Lucas tried to assure him that the news came from German sources.

'I let you snoop around Russia once before at great risk to myself just because once you saved my life,' argued Zhdanov. 'Why should I take this risk again? I shall have you watched every instant of your stay, so tread very carefully.'

Then six days later, Ribbentrop's private plane, *Grenzmark*, arrived at Moscow airport and Lucas stood by the Kremlin gate as the Reich's Foreign Minister was driven through in his car. Beside Lucas a British colonel, one of the military mission who had been patiently waiting for some weeks in the hope of an agreement with the Kremlin, made the barely audible comment: 'Tho blasted Germans!'

Gradually Lucas discovered what Stalin's immediate aims were behind this facade of a German–Soviet Pact. First, he wished to acquire more territory and thus put more space between the USSR and the decadent and imperialistic lands of Europe. His prime target was Bessarabia, on Poland's eastern side, an area where there were many Russians, certain land on both sides of the Pripet Marshes and a strip of territory linking Poland with Latvia. He needed those vital lands under Soviet control for defence purposes in case Germany ever decided to march against Russia. Following that, his aim was to annexe Latvia and Esthonia and strategic points in Finland.

Lucas's main source of information was Aloysha, the interpreter, who was present at the only conference between Stalin and Ribbentrop. This proved to be vital for our super-spy's purpose, for while the text of the Pact was officially released, and there were reputed to be no secret clauses, there was in fact a purely oral understanding between the Soviet leader and the German Foreign Secretary. Aloysha guessed what that understanding was. A huge map of eastern Europe was spread out on a table and on this Stalin drew a line around the areas in which he insisted Soviet influence must be supreme. From certain nods, marks on the map, gestures and brief words, it was clear that this was tacitly agreed upon between them.

Until this period Lucas had been inclined to believe that there were people inside the British Establishment, who were all for appeasing Germany and keeping out of a world war by allowing that nation to turn on Russia alone. He still felt that there might be a few who thought along those lines, but at last it dawned on him that this story had been grossly magnified by

Soviet and German agents, not merely to cause mischief, but also to pave the way for a German–Soviet Pact. That was why — while an Allied military mission spent three months in Russia trying unsuccessfully to come to some agreement — Ribbentrop was able to bring off a deal in less than three hours.

As soon after this as possible Lucas left Russia and made his way into Finland. At least that was his story to Wythe Williams, but it may well have been a "cover". Certainly his information was airmailed from Helsinki just before censorship was introduced. His news was that Hitler would attack Poland within a day or two, that there would be brave words from the British and French about saving Poland, but that Williams must 'not be fooled by them. No help will come. The Poles are doomed, whether they know it or not.'[10]

In the meantime Lucas seems to have passed on information not merely to Wythe Williams, but to Britain as well. Some of this was certainly sent by way of Switzerland where he had a number of trusted contacts. "Roger" is still convinced that the man he knew as either "Walter" or "Werther" was Lucas, and that a message he received via a third party was from Lucas himself.

'Lucas must have known I had close contacts with the British, as well as others, and decided I was the safest person to use to pass on the information. Why, you may ask, did he not use other channels? He certainly had his own contacts in British Intelligence. I believe the answer is that by that time he had begun to mistrust British Intelligence, or at least certain people in London with whom he had had dealings. Not only did he believe that some of them were serving the Soviet cause, but that they had tried to smear his reputation in America.'

Certainly, various documents sent from British MI6 to the Federal Bureau of Investigation make it clear that an enemy of Lucas's inside that organization had set out, even before World War II, to cast doubts on his good intentions. No allegations against him were made from the British side (at least not in writing), but the underlying suggestion was that Lucas needed to be watched carefully, that much more required to be known about him and that his travels in certain areas were not always easily explained. Indeed, they were not! In his own way Lucas had begun to play a game as dangerous as anything Sidney

Reilly had ever attempted. To slip in and out of Soviet Russia and Germany, at such a time, with a European background but American nationality, was inevitably to court suspicion in some quarters. Lucas was a crusading, free-lance spy, unaffiliated to any single intelligence service. This phenomenon is always liable to be unfairly suspected.

The next communication which Williams received from Lucas came some weeks later in a letter post-marked Rio de Janeiro. It was sent to Williams' private address and had not been censored. The truly astonishing quality about Lucas' gift for writing was the ease with which he would slip into the vernacular of the language in which he was writing at any given moment. This letter started off, 'Dear Wythe, How're tricks in your orchard? I understand that, with the phoney war, you in the United States read daily reports that Hitler is practically through and does not know which way to turn. Don't believe one word of it.'

Lucas was in fact seriously concerned about American newspapers getting a totally wrong impression as to how the war was going, especially with some of the ridiculously optimistic comments that, as there was no more fighting (Poland had been overrun long before), the war would 'be over by Christmas.' He was disgusted with the way in which the correspondents of American newspapers were being fed a totally false picture of events not only in Paris, but in London, too. In France some of these correspondents were being taken on conducted tours of the Maginot Line where they would be lulled into complacency not by any emphasis on armaments, but on how well the soldiers there were being looked after during the "Phoney War" period, the abundance of food and wine, entertainments and games for the troops.

Lucas' comment on all this was, 'I wish to God that the French would run short on wines and actors and overstock with tanks, guns and planes. But what's the use of hoping . . .?'

Since arriving in Germany once again he had had a few problems. On his way into that country he had been detained for two days in Sassnitz, though no reason was given, and apparently he had visited Stockholm too. He found that examinations at frontier posts were much more rigorous and that there were far more questions asked. He even had to invent a

76

plausible story about his visit to Russia, for his relative in Germany, the alibi being that he had to help another relative who was seriously ill. To get any real details of Hitler's next plans, he knew that he had to keep close to the relative he called Eugen in the household staff at Berchtesgaden.

"Roger" has an interesting comment to make on this move by Lucas. 'I think he had come to realize that the only way he could get absolutely foolproof intelligence from any side was by concentrating on the inner ranks of each, that is both in Russia and Germany. I was told by another colleague, a member of PAKBO (our own anti-fascist organization), that "Werther" doesn't really trust us. He would like to trust us, he wishes us well, but he told me that in the ranks of the anti-fascists there are too many communist conspirators who would betray us at the drop of a hat. For a while he tried to make contact with the *Funfergruppen* (Groups of Five), a series of five-men communist cells inside Germany which were to undermine the Nazi movement by quiet propaganda and subversion of one kind or another. It all sounded wonderful, but it never achieved anything worthwhile, it was doomed by the Nazi Soviet Pact. In any case it had long since been "blown" by one of its own people.'

Was "Roger's" deduction correct? The answer to this, almost certainly in the affirmative, lies in an article which appeared in Britain's *New Statesman & Nation* in August 1933. This was called *The Revolutionary Movement in Nazi Germany* (*Funfergruppen*), and the editor, Kingsley Martin, wrote 'This article based on intimate knowledge of the situation in Germany, throws light on a movement whose activities are known to few foreigners and probably to only a minority of Germans.' If anyone "blew" the secret of the *Funfergruppen*, it was Kingsley Martin, that devious fellow-traveller who did so much harm in so many ways.

How could it help such a movement in Nazi Germany where the power of the Gestapo was omnipresent, if such details could be spelt out in a British periodical? Mr Robin Bruce Lockhart, the son of Sir Robert Bruce Lockhart who knew Sidney Reilly, has written: 'Although relating to Germany, the articles were an invitation to the magazine's readers to copy the German, and form secret, subversive five-man communist "cells". Rostovsky/Henri [this refers to the author of the article who wrote under the pseudonym Ernst Henri, though his real name was Simeyon Rostovsky] was subtly following up Reilly's view that the Soviets should not confine their recruiting activities in Britain to the working classes but concentrate on gaining secret adherents among those members of the 'Establishment' who were politically inclined to the left.[11]

Lucas had seen these articles, he knew all about Rostovsky, and he realized that some in the communist hierarchy were quite prepared to betray and sacrifice one of their own networks, if it was not succeeding, by using it to encourage others in other countries to attempt the same ploy, but under much safer conditions. One message which he passed through to "Roger" was: 'Beware! That article by Rostovsky shows you cannot trust the Communists when they start something off. If their plan fails, they won't hesitate to betray its existence in order to persuade some other bloke to try it out in another country. I shall from now on deeply suspect any news of Cells of Five, and try to find out who their members are, because you can be sure they are as much our enemies as the Nazis or the Fascists.'

8

"MOLES" IN THE GESTAPO

In Berchestgaden Lucas boldly offered to help his relative in Hitler's entourage with any work he had to cope with. It was a reasonable suggestion because when Hitler was at his Bavarian retreat many routine chores had to wait while secret sessions were held, which meant that work for the staff began to pile up. Then suddenly Hitler would go away for a long spell, the whole atmosphere would change and Lucas would find he could move around much more freely. So many top figures had left the Berghof that the ranks of the Gestapo and the Schutz-taffel officers were also diminished. In these circumstances Lucas was not only able to glean more information, but to make new contacts inside the household.

At first what he gleaned was little more than backstairs gossip, which was not altogether without interest even if it did not fill Lucas's need for vital war intelligence. There was for example a story of a rift between Hitler and his alleged mistress, Eva Braun. Some at the Berghof told Lucas that these two were secretly married, but that Hitler insisted that Eva should never be referred to as Frau Hitler. Yet he came across no evidence of anything other than a somewhat mysteri-ous platonic relationship: they never even shared the same bedroom. However, Hitler was noticeably happier when Eva was around, so news of a rift and the fact that Eva was supposed to have gone off to Munich seemed to some to spell trouble.

Lucas's first acquisition of an agent inside the Berghof, apart from his relative, was the man he called Gottlieb, the man of whom he had said to Williams 'he is in the Gestapo, but not of it. Many of the Berghof staff are Gestapo agents whose duty it is to spy on those close to Hitler — also on each other — and report to Gestapo Chief Himmler.... Gottlieb is one of these men.'[1]

Gottlieb himself came from a Bavarian family who had seen their wealth disappear in the post-war inflation. He had joined the Hitler movement in 1929 and eventually entered the Gestapo under Reinhard Heydrich, then chief of the Berlin branch of that service. Not surprisingly, while serving under such a hated man as Heydrich, he developed doubts about the whole movement, not least when he discovered how faked and planted evidence was used to round people up. There was also another reason why Gottlieb was critical of Nazism deep down in his heart: for two years he had studied in the United States and he began to wonder whether Germany might not be happier under an American style of constitution.

Lucas's next recruit from within the ranks of the Berghof was the woman referred to before as both "Clara" and "Olga". She was even more important than Gottlieb because she had access to copies of all documents signed by Hitler himself, and, as we have seen, had her own reasons to dislike the Nazis. Her secret marriage with an aide to Captain Ernst Roehm, the chief of the SA, or Storm Troops, had resulted in her pregnancy. When, on the night of 30 June 1934, Hitler stamped out the whole of the Roehm faction, Clara's husband was among those killed. Clara dared not even attend his funeral, such was the threat hanging over all associated with Roehm. She had to keep the pregnancy secret for fear of being forced to reveal the identity of the father, yet she needed her job at Berchtesgaden so she got permission for a long holiday, went to Switzerland where her child was born, and left the baby in charge of a Swiss peasant family.

Here Lucas was lucky. Clara's problem was sending money to Switzerland for her baby without the German authorities finding out. Once he knew this, Lucas had no difficulty in suggesting a solution: he could switch his dollars into his Swiss bank account and she could repay him in German marks. From then onwards Lucas and Clara shared mutual secrets.

Meanwhile Lucas managed to organize a visit for himself to the Skoda munitions works, and was deeply impressed with what they were producing — 'I stood at the end of the assembly line and saw five-ton steel monsters coming out, one every forty five minutes.... But what amazed me most were the nine-inch mobile siege guns with long barrels, mounted on tractors. I never knew this could be done. I understand that these were the guns that were used to blast Warsaw to bits. I just wonder if the French have the faintest idea of what they will be called upon to face.'[2]

Lucas was no longer in any doubt that the war would continue following the defeat of Poland. If Britain and France made no attempt to hit back at Germany he felt certain that Hitler would call their bluff and seek further conquests. Otherwise, he told himself, why should a score or more of anti-aircraft guns have been brought up to the Berghof together with huge searchlights and listening devices. What worried him was that the newspapers of the free world gave no hint of impending disaster and he was horrified by a British radio commentary which spoke of a gradually developing revolution against Hitler within Germany. The Allies, he decided, would defeat themselves with their own complacent propaganda.

He passed on to Williams an address in Switzerland through which he could be contacted, but insisted that there must be no reference to Berchtesgaden. Before Wythe could respond a stranger called at his office at *Greenwich Time*, asked to see him personally, gave him a bulky envelope and left abruptly. Once again there was a missive from Lucas.

This latest report was to let *Greenwich Time* know that their roving correspondent had fixed up two new informants as well as from Gottlieb and Clara. One of these, code-named Wolfgang, was enlisted through Clara. Wolfgang, Lucas explained, could be tremendously useful, but there was a hazard. He was passionately in love with Clara and very jealous. He did not know about Clara's child in Switzerland and Lucas sincerely hoped that, if Wolfgang found out about it, he would not suspect Lucas — who had visited the child and even given it some toys — of being the father. If that happened it could end everything.

The one vital hold Lucas had on Wolfgang was his knowledge that Wolfgang lived at Fuschl Castle, near Salzburg. Wolfgang's father had been arrested and executed for some obscure reason and Joachim von Ribbentrop had stolen the estate for himself. Wolfgang was convinced that the Nazis were behind the elimination of his father, but, always hoping that one day by some miracle he might see Fuschl Castle restored to its rightful owner (in his own view, himself), he stayed on there as a member of Ribbentrop's staff.

Thus Lucas had Clara at Hitler's headquarters; Wolfgang at Ribbentrop's estate; "Manfred", who was also serving in the Gestapo in Berlin and was a friend of Gottlieb; Zhdanov and Aloysha in Moscow; Tito in Yugoslavia (if he could ever get there); three contacts in Switzerland and at least four elsewhere. This gave Wythe Williams a network of correspondents far better than any he could have acquired himself, even with substantial financial backing.

From these sources Lucas had been given vague hints that both Russia and Germany had a spy inside the American Embassy in London. This was the kind of story which he could not hope to get published, but he was desperately anxious to pass it on as a warning to a reliable source in the Allied camp. The more he listened to such stories and weighed them up the more he believed that there was only one spy in the US Embassy, a person who had connections with both regimes, Nazi and Communist. Only two names occurred to him as possibilities: Tyler Kent, who was working in the cipher department of the US Embassy in London, and a White Russian named Anatoly Baykalov. In the end he decided to pay greater attention to Tyler Kent because he had learned that he was previously posted to Moscow and had very close Russian friends. It was not until the following year that Kent was unmasked by the British as having passed intelligence to the Germans, and that the American Embassy in London waived diplomatic immunity and allowed Kent to be tried and sentenced to prison.

Kent had previously served in the American Embassy in Moscow, but he was not charged with being a double agent during his trial. Only then was Lucas's hunch about a spy working for both the Germans and the Soviets fully confirmed. Tyler Kent's name was undoubtedly on one of the lists of potential Soviet supporters among American citizens which Lucas managed to glimpse when he was in Moscow in 1939. What puzzled Lucas when he heard of Kent's arrest by the British was why MI5 had taken so long to inform the Americans of their suspicions about him. If Lucas was puzzled, the reaction of Herschal V. Johnson, the US Counsellor, was one of outrage. When he heard that MI5 had identified Tyler Kent as a security risk eight months before they had advised the US Embassy, he stated: 'It was most regrettable that Scotland Yard had not informed us of these circumstances at the time. We would never have left the man in the code room if there had been the slightest suspicion against him.'

Had Moscow as well as Berlin been getting details of top secret messages passing through the US Embassy? Lucas suspected that they had, and that this might even have happened with the connivance of someone in the British counter-espionage service, one who was a friend of Baykalov.

Lucas was still in Germany when the attempt on Hitler's life was made on 8 November 1939. Eight members of the Nazi Party were killed and sixty-three others injured in an explosion which wrecked the beer cellar in which Hitler and his comrades were celebrating the anniversary of the Munich putsch of 1923. The bomb exploded slightly less than twenty minutes after Hitler had finished his speech and left, together with his senior Party members. Luckily for Lucas one of his informants was present at the party and escaped injury.

Immediately, the Nazi Propaganda Ministry put out the story that this explosion was the work of British agents who had deliberately sought to kill the Fuhrer. The truth, as Lucas discovered, was that the incident was deliberately staged by Goering and Himmler. The Nazi hierarchy had been dismayed to learn that after the victory over Poland there was an almost overwhelming desire among the German people, even including some Nazis, for a move for peace. The bomb was used as a means of rallying support around Hitler and restoring faith in the necessity of carrying on with the war. Arrangements were made in advance for Hitler and his immediate party to leave before it was due to explode.

These were difficult days for Wythe Williams. Not only had he to consider the risks of prophesying German intentions, he also needed to safeguard Lucas while he was still inside Germany. Lucas seems to have relied entirely upon Williams' discretion when it came to publishing his information. There were a few days on which Williams would become alarmed, more for his friend than himself. One such was when he was interviewed by a feature writer eager to know what his sources were. Somewhat rashly Williams indicated that he had 'a few spies in key places.' When the interview was published he was represented as having a network of spies all over Europe and for some weeks afterwards the repercussions of this article gave him awkward and anxious moments.

Both *Greenwich Time* and Williams' radio broadcasts seem to have attracted widespread attention as their forecasts were repeatedly proved correct. Nevertheless Williams was for a long time regarded as a scaremonger and self-publicist, which was very unfair. The trouble was that the refugees from Nazi Germany who flocked into the United States gave a distorted picture of events. They stressed the horrors of the Gestapo and Hitler's brown-shirted thugs, but then tried to make out that Hitler was actually hated by the great mass of Germans who would be only too eager to topple him at the right moment. This was, of course, far from the truth as Hitler was — rightly in many ways — looked upon as the man who had rescued Germany from the economic chaos of the 1920's. Such re-assuring misinformation did a lot of harm when taken up by the media. It made people imagine that Hitler would soon disappear from the political scene.

From time to time the same mysterious messenger arrived either at Williams' home or his office with a package of material from Lucas. He declined to give his name or say anything about himself. Nor was he named in *Secret Sources* when it was published. But in a review of that book in the *New York Times* S.T. Williamson wrote that 'the reports, which compose the bulk of the book, with running comment by Mr Williams, were brought to this country by Klaus Mann, a tight-lipped and somewhat grasping person who shuttled on mysterious business between Germany and the United States, apparently with the knowledge and consent of our State Department.'[3]

There were occasional references in *Secret Sources* to a somewhat mysterious character known as Klausmann, but no special linking to Klaus Mann. The true identity of Klaus

Mann was that he was the son of Thomas Mann, the eminent German author and zealous anti-Nazi crusader who fled to the United States shortly after Hitler's take-over. Thomas Mann had three children, Heinrich, Erika and Klaus. Klaus was born in 1906 and it would seem that he and Erika eventually fled to the US and carried on their anti-nazi campaign during the war. That is, however, a somewhat vague report from Intelligence sources, totally lacking in any follow-up. But Bernard Yudain has this comment to make on Klaus Mann: 'During World War II I was a member of the staff of *Stars and Stripes* (Mediterranean). I wasn't with the paper during its start-up. By the time I joined, *S. & S.* was well established in both Naples and Rome (where I worked) and later I went on to head a one-man bureau in Leghorn. A member of that staff was Klaus Mann, I saw him seldom and had but a passing relationship so I don't know the circumstances or the time he became a staffer. I know he died in 1949 and am almost certain (it needs checking) that he was a suicide.'[4]

One of Lucas's early contacts in Britain was Vera Alexandrovna Guchkova, the only daughter of A.I. Guchkov who had been a leader of the Octobrists Party which wanted limited constitutional reforms in Czarist Russia. Later he was War Minister in the Provisional Government and political leader of the "Whites" in the civil war. When the revolution succeeded and the Bolsheviks took over, Vera escaped from Russia with her parents. She was somewhat of a rebel, as well as an extremely attractive girl, but the story that she shocked her family by joining the French Communist Party because they regarded this as an act of betrayal can be dismissed. Her father was as devious a figure as any who ever mixed in Russian politics and later he was one of the leading figures in Berlin who helped to sponsor the undercover Soviet organization, The Trust.

Vera Guchkova divorced her first husband, Count Peter Shelig, and married Robert Trail, a Communist and celebrated oarsman of King's College, Cambridge, later killed in the Spanish Civil War. Lucas kept in touch with her through his occasional meetings with Professor Pigou, also of King's College, on the latter's mountaineering expeditions to Switzerland. It was with somewhat of a shock that Lucas learned on

85

one of his visits to Russia that Vera had returned there in the late 1930's with a small band of liberal sympathisers to the Russian cause. She, like the rest of them, had doubts about Stalin and how he was leading the country, but she had a deep love of her homeland.

Fortunately for Vera, Lucas was able to tip her off only hours before she was due to be arrested by the NKVD. It has been said that it was Yezhov himself, then head of the NKVD, who had tipped her off, but in fact it was Lucas, who had been given the news of Vera's impending arrest by someone in the Zhdanov camp. She escaped back to France, but was arrested on the outbreak of war, along with other Communists, and kept in internment. Eventually she managed to get back to London in 1941.

Vera had been one of Lucas's informants during the 1930's. She lived until the age of eighty, mainly at Cambridge in her later years, still holding court with her admirers and friends who included both Stalin's daughter and relatives of the last of the Tsars.

"Clara", or "Olga" was the most important of Lucas's agents in the Berghof. She worked on a vast quantity of files which were situated close to a ventilator through which she could sometimes hear what the Fuhrer was being told. 'What he is being told and what he is actually thinking can be matters on which conjecture is extremely risky,' she once warned Lucas. 'I can tell you what he is told, but he often keeps his real thoughts to himself. He loves to act swiftly, to bark out orders, but beneath it all is sometimes a surprisingly insecure man.'

During his stay in Germany Lucas did not spend all his time at Berchtesgaden. He also had contacts which enabled him to visit Karin Hall, Marshal Goering's own estate, and he spent some time in Berlin. On at least two or three occasions he found himself forced to click his heels and give the Nazi salute. As he said afterwards: 'One does these things if one wishes to keep alive.'

One factor helped Lucas in his meetings with some of the Nazi hierarchy: he had held the rank of lieutenant-colonel in the armies fighting the Bolsheviks which, despite the Nazi–Soviet Pact, was still something the Nazis respected, so he was frequently addressed as '*Herr Oberstleutnant*'. More often than not, it helped if he was accompanied by some attractive *fraulein* who was a Nazi Party member. One such was Liese, an attractive blonde with clear blue eyes, but with a mind faster-working than most. Liese knew "Clara" (or "Olga") and all about her child in Switzerland. Her father had been a Nazi Party official, but then surprisingly was said to have committed suicide. Liese never believed this verdict on his death and felt certain that in some way he had been liquidated. But, with the emphasis on the need to conform, or at least to seem to conform, she pretended to accept it.

Shortly afterwards Liese found herself with a post in Goering's secretariat at Karin Hall. Not only did she have access to official files and dossiers, she was also brought forward on social occasions to entertain guests on account of her looks and charm. From Lucas' viewpoint Liese was in a perfect position to pass on to him a wealth of inside information and a great deal of worthwhile gossip. There were hints of dissension between Ribbentrop and Count Ciano, the Italian Foreign Secretary, over the Nazi–Soviet Pact, which was highly unpopular in mainly Catholic Italy. Snippets of gossip also suggested that Goering was critical of Ribbentrop's arrangements with Stalin on the grounds that in view of the Russian attack on Finland it was impossible for the Germans to intervene successfully to check this invasion. Ribbentrop insisted that the pact ruled out any question of German aid for the Finns. It was obvious that there was disagreement, too, on the question of the division of Poland between Russia and Germany. General (later Field-Marshal) Walther von Brauchitsch had gone to see Hitler personally to complain that the idea of the Vistula River being the dividing line between the two occupying powers was 'a gross military nonsense and a political error:' he wanted the dividing line to be the River Bug. Finally it became necessary for Ribbentrop to make a second trip to Moscow, this time to agree to Russia taking control of Lithuania, but with Germany acquiring and retaining all the lands between the Vistula and Bug rivers.

Karin Hall proved to be an admirable listening-post at this time and Liese (Lucas gave her the code-name of "Linda") was an invaluable source on policy-making. Once again the story was circulated in Karin Hall that there was a strong group of Ministers in the Chamberlain Government who formed a "peace party", or at least the equivalent of one. This included R.A. Butler (by nature an appeaser of almost anything and anyone from dictators to the British public), Sir John Simon, and that intriguing civil servant, Sir Horace Wilson. Both Goering and Goebbels were convinced that this "peace party" could be exploited by clever propaganda, using Mussolini as an intermediary (Italy was not then at war), suggesting that Germany's war machine was weak and that a peace deal satisfactory to all was still possible. This worried Lucas a great deal and he did his utmost to pass on a warning about such plans.

Having failed to be taken seriously by Britain's Secret Service chiefs, Lucas had made his number one target for the receipt of information on German plans no less than Sir Robert Vansittart in the British Foreign Office. Lucas knew that in Vansittart he had an ally, but, unfortunately, one he did not know personally. He knew that Vansittart had made it clear long before this that Germany's political plans included not merely the absorption of Austria, Czechoslovakia, Eupen and Malmedy, Schleswig and the Polish part of Upper Silesia and Transylvania, but that he had also warned that their plans extended to 'territorial annexation of Poland and Russia, including the conquest of the Ukraine and complete control of the Baltic states.'[5]

Lucas tried to have messages passed via Switzerland to Professor Pigou at Cambridge in the hope that Pigou would pass these on to Vansittart, but there is no evidence as to whether such information ever reached Vansittart, whose papers reveal no clue on the matter. It is possible that the messages were passed on, but with an embargo on the name of the informant, as Lucas was still highly dubious of giving too much away, fearing the backlash of either some appeasing element in British officialdom, or, worse still, a pro-Soviet faction such as he believed had helped pave the way for the killing of Krivitsky. Lucas was well aware that his friends in Switzerland were probably linked, if only unofficially, to a Soviet network.

What worried Lucas most was the fact that he knew from what he had learned both at Berchtesgaden and Karin Hall that right up to the end of July 1939, the British Government was still secretly trying to make a deal with Germany which would allow that nation a free hand in Eastern Europe in exchange for some vague peace deal in the West. This much he had gleaned from information on talks between Dirksen, the German Ambassador in London, and Wohltaht, a Nazi official used on various overseas missions. Sir Horace Wilson, who took part in these talks, stressed to Dirksen that the talks were 'highly confidential . . . and that if anything about them were to leak out there would be a great scandal and Chamberlain would probably be forced to resign.' At the same time Dirksen was assured that the talks going on with the USSR 'were only a subsidiary means, which would cease to be operative as soon as agreement with Germany, the all-important objective worth striving for, had been really attained.'[6]

Not surprisingly, Lucas began to lose much faith in the British resolution to stand up to the Nazis at this time, even after war had been declared, though he felt that with the right leader, such as Churchill, the situation could be changed. To pass his warnings to British Intelligence he had to rely to some extent on those intermediaries who were either pro-Soviet, or in Soviet intelligence networks, official or unofficial. This he continued to do, risky and difficult as it was, despite the fact that his major target was the American people whom he hoped to awake to a realization of how ultimately their own way of life could be threatened.

THE SWISS CONNECTION

"Olga", also known as "Clara", was the chief intermediary in all this. She had managed to establish, through Lucas's guidance, contacts not only with some inside the Soviet-controlled "Lucy" ring, but with PAKBO and INSA networks, too. It was through these contacts that "Roger" picked up the importance of "Olga". 'We knew she was an ally of "Werther" as we called van Narvig, Lucas, or whatever his name was,' said "Roger," 'and for that reason we placed great reliance on her intelligence, some of which was passed to the Russians.' There is still much speculation, argument and disagreement about how the "Lucy" network got all its intelligence. Today it is fashionable to say that none came from official British circles: that is totally untrue. Quite a lot of approved British intelligence, including some deciphering of German signals was passed on to "Lucy", but at the same time "Lucy" probably did as well with information gained from unofficial, anti-fascist organizations such as PAKBO and INSA as from its own agents. Some of the latter led far too easy a life in Switzerland to be all that useful, and made up for their own lack of intelligence-gathering by borrowing or acquiring information from other organizations.

'I should like to make it quite clear,' added "Roger", 'that in no way was "Olga" working for the Soviets and there was absolutely no connection between her and the chief Soviet female spy in Switzerland at that time, Ruth Kuczynski. "Olga" would never have been trusted by the Soviet apparat however much she might wish to help the anti-fascist cause.'

"Lucy" was the Soviet organization which the British Alexander Foote joined when he arrived in Switzerland. Foote had

(Murnor Studio, Florida)

William Van Narvig, alias William D. Lucas, the freelance spy who has baffled most secret services. This is the only reputed photograph ever taken of him c. 1945-50.

Left

Andrei Zhdanov, Secretary-General of the Russian Communist Party and once regarded as the probable successor to Stalin. Lucas once saved his life.

Professor Arthur Pigou of King's College, Cambridge, a friend of William Lucas and a link in his communications system.

Marshal Tito playing chess with his Chief of Staff. Lucas knew him as 'Comrade Antonio' and other code-names.

Right

Sidney Reilly, quadruple agent, whose loyalties shifted from country to country.

Hitler, Professor Albert Speer, Minister of Munitions, and Fritz Todt, on the terrace of the Berghof in Bavaria. It was behind these windows that Lucas had a spy to listen in to conversations.

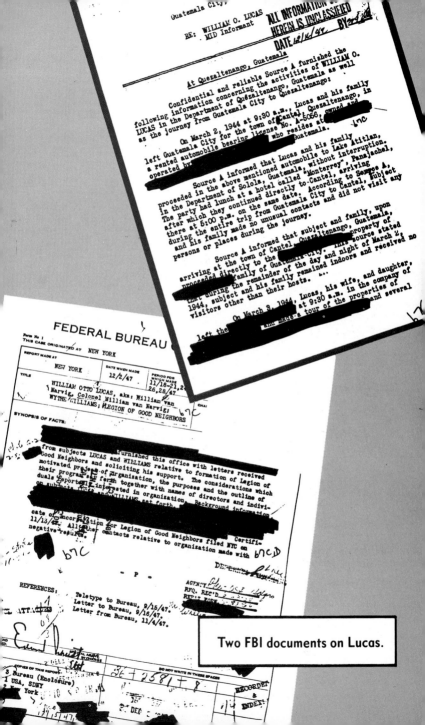

Guatemala City,

RE: WILLIAM O. LUCAS
MID Informant

ALL INFORMATION
HEREIN IS UNCLASSIFIED
DATE 12/16/47 BY ___

At Quezaltenango, Guatemala

Confidential and reliable Source A furnished the following information concerning the activities of WILLIAM O. LUCAS in the Department of Quezaltenango, Guatemala as well as the journey from Guatemala City to Quezaltenango.

On March 2, 1944 at 9:30 a.m., Lucas and his family left Guatemala City for the town of Cantel, Quezaltenango, in a rented automobile bearing license No. A-5056, owned and operated by ███████ who resides at ███████ Guatemala.

Source A informed that Lucas and his family proceeded in the above mentioned automobile to Lake Atitlan, in the Department of Solola, Guatemala, without interruption. The party had lunch at a hotel called "Monterrey", Panajachel, after which they continued directly to Cantel, arriving there at 5:00 p.m. on the same date. According to Source A, during the entire trip from Guatemala City to Cantel, subject and his family made no unusual contacts and did not visit any persons or places during the journey.

Source A informed that subject and family, upon arriving at the town of Cantel, Quezaltenango, Guatemala, proceeded directly to the ███████ This ██████ property of ██████ family of Guatemala City. This source stated that during the remainder of the day and night of March 2 1944, subject and his family remained indoors and received no visitors other than their hosts.

On March 3, 1944, at 9:30 a.m. in the company of ██████, Lucas, his wife, and daughter, left the ██████ and made a tour of the properties of ██████ and several

---

FEDERAL BUREAU

Form No 1
THIS CASE ORIGINATED AT NEW YORK

REPORT MADE AT: NEW YORK

DATE WHEN MADE: 12/2/47

PERIOD FOR WHICH MADE: 11/18-21,2, 26,28/47

TITLE: WILLIAM OTTO LUCAS, aka: William van Narvig, Colonel William van Narvig; WYTHE WILLIAMS; LEGION OF GOOD NEIGHBORS

SYNOPSIS OF FACTS:

██████ furnished this office with letters received from subjects LUCAS and WILLIAMS relative to formation of Legion of Good Neighbors and soliciting his support. The considerations which motivated project of organization, the purposes and the outline of their program set forth together with names of directors and individuals reportedly interested in organization. Background information on subjects WILLIAMS set forth. ██████ Certificate of incorporation for Legion of Good Neighbors filed NYC on 11/13/47. All other contacts relative to organization made with negative results.

- P -

REFERENCES:
Teletype to Bureau, 9/15/47.
Letter to Bureau, 9/16/47.
Letter from Bureau, 11/4/47.

COPIES OF THIS REPORT
3 Bureau (Enclosure)
1 USA, SDNY
York

Two FBI documents on Lucas.

(Popperfoto)

Gerhard Eisler, German-born No. 1 Communist in the USA, being forcibly removed from the Polish liner *Batory* by Scotland Yard officers to await extradition to New York in 1949.

Rudolf Roessler, a key member of the 'Lucy' network in World War II, who in 1953 was sentenced to a year's imprisonment for selling Western defence secrets to Czechoslovakia.

Alexander Foote, a spy who came in from the cold.

been recruited after his service in the British Battalion of the International Brigade in the Spanish Civil War by none other than Douglas Springhall, a key man in the Communist Party. Foote had this to say about his recruitment: 'The man in charge of the formation of the battalion was Wilfred McCartney. The political commisar was Douglas Springhall, who played a more vital part in my life later when he recruited me for the Red Army Intelligence.[1]

Rather more interesting, however, is what Foote said on the subject of why he became a Soviet spy. 'I think I can say, speaking for myself and my colleagues, that the mercenary motive was subsidiary,' he wrote. 'Patriotism was obviously not applicable.... Nor can it be said that in every case idealism was a primary cause. It was certainly not so in my case, *since it was some time before I realized for whom I was working* [this author's italics]. Many conversations that I have had since with others who were "in the net" have shown that they, too, at first had little idea — if any — of the identity of their masters, save that it was for the Communist ideal as a whole, which is, after all, the vaguest sort of master to have. In my case I was recruited out of the dark into the dark — a sort of blind catch-as-catch-can — and went into the arena of international espionage with my eyes open, but open under a black bandage. I knew I was a spy and knew against whom I was supposed to be spying [in Foote's case mainly against Germany], but at first had no idea of the why and wherefore or of the directing hand.'[2]

Foote wrote this after he had returned voluntarily to Britain and confessed to all he had done. For that reason alone it seems to be a reasonable account of how Britons of the day were lured into the service of the USSR. How many similar agents of British citizenship were engaged without their knowing in the beginning just who was pushing them, or who was controlling them? Even in the case of Alexander Foote it was not Springhall's recommendation alone. Foote had gone to Spain in December 1936, not as a Party member but certainly vouched for by members of the Party. His motive for volunteering for the International Brigade was that of wishing to stop the march of fascism in Europe. When after a spell as a transport officer in Spain, Foote returned to Britain, he understood he was to be courier between the CPGB headquarters in

King Street and the International Brigade, under the guise of a
Red Cross driver. But when he got to King Street he soon
discovered that the Comintern had other ideas for him. He was
recruited for what he was told would be "a very dangerous
assignment" by Fred Copeman, the liaison officer for selected
agents of the GRU. Foote was vague about Copeman's actual
status, believing him to be on the fringe of the Soviet net, used
by Springhall and others as an innocent cover for their contact
work. This may well have been the case for, whereas
Springhall was until his death a dedicated Communist,
Copeman had a change of mind. Like Springhall, Copeman
had also been in the Royal Navy, having been discharged for
his part in the Invergordon Mutiny. He then joined the CPGB
and eventually went to Spain to join the International Brigade.
By 1939 he was managing the International Brigade's
Dependents' Aid Fund, but he quarrelled with his colleagues at
King Street as to how its finances should be run, eventually
joining the Oxford Group and defecting from the Party.

One interesting factor emerges about the various rendezvous
points for recruitment at this time: they nearly all centred
around the West Hampstead, Maida Vale, St John's Wood
district. Both "Kim" Philby and James Klugmenn, another
Party activist, lived in Hampstead. Foote stated that Copeman
told him to go to an address in St John's Wood where he
received instructions from the 'respectable housewife with a
slight foreign accent who interviewed me.' When Foote
returned to Britain after World War II he made his home in
Clifton Gardens, Maida Vale, and soon found that some
members of the Soviet apparat were still in the area, including
'a sister of SONIA [code-name for Ruth Kuczynski of the
"Lucy" ring in Switzerland] a ... one-time member of the
Hampstead CP who had a knowledge of my collaboration with
her sister in the Swiss network'.[3]

"Roger" described the three or four apparats as all anti-
fascist, but 'dangerously overlapping one another.' 'One was
never quite sure who was with us or against us, or to what
extent the Germans had infiltrated at least one of our
networks. You must remember, too, that some of us were
deeply alarmed after the assassination of Ignace Reiss by the
NKVD inside Switzerland. He had been a key Soviet intelli-

gence officer. For two years prior to the war, while there were less than thirty-five full-time agents of the USSR in Germany, there were more than fifty in Switzerland. And suddenly the whole set-up in Switzerland was threatened with a great shake-out.'

Arthur Koestler, a former Communist who had begun to be disillusioned with the Party shortly before World War II, originally became a party member in Berlin under the alias of Ivan Sternberg. After a trip to Moscow he went to Hungary where, he said, he was not known as a Communist. There he met Alexander (Sandor) Rado, a former Austro–Hungarian officer who had become a GRU agent. As a cover Rado (code-name "Dora") set up a press agency in Paris, employing Koestler as one of his two writers. Eventually Rado was transferred to Switzerland as regional director of the Soviet network in that country about 1936–37. There were great advantages in making Switzerland a major base for espionage operations — its traditional neutrality in wartime, the fact that the neutrality laws meant there was no discrimination against any country and that, if anything, the Swiss preferred to turn a blind eye to espionage rather than to act against a foreign power.

Foote's account of his recruitment into the GRU, and the instructions given to him in Maida Vale, reads hilariously like a spy fiction spoof. He was to present himself 'outside the General Post Office in Geneva ... I was to be wearing a white scarf and to be holding in my right hand a leather belt. As the clock struck noon I would be approached by a woman carrying a string shopping bag containing a green parcel; she would be holding an orange in her hand ... The woman would ask me, in English, where I had bought the belt, and I was to reply that I had bought it in an ironmonger's shop in Paris. Then I was to ask where I could buy an orange like hers and she was to say I could have hers for an English penny.'[4]

The woman he met at the Geneva GPO was none other than "Sonia", alias Ursula-Maria Hamburger, alias Beurton, but now more generally known under her family name of Ursula Ruth Kuczynski, whose father was a German Jewish professor of economics at Oxford University. Under her present name of Ruth Werner she has published her own story, *Sonja's Rapport*, from her home in East Berlin in 1977. It was after she had attended a course at the Wireless Communications School in Moscow that she was promoted from the rank of Captain in the Soviet GRU to that of major, later rising to lieutenant-colonel. She was sent to Switzerland to set up home in a villa at Caux high above Montreux, having been ordered to rebuild the Swiss network after the Stalinist purge, with the full backing of Sandor Rado. There were some fifty agents in the network, including four Britons. Soon it possessed three transmitting stations, one of which was operated by Foote (code-name "Jim") and another by an underground British Communist named Bill Phillips (code-name "Jack"). Both Foote and Phillips were used for forays into Germany, hazardous operations at this time. Of Phillips, Foote stated that 'he had worked with me in Brigade transport in Spain... he, too, was not a Party member ... Bill had already set himself up in Frankfurt, having received instructions as vague and as unsatisfactory as mine.'[5]

The two men received their initial training from "Sonia" (Kuczynski). Foote proved to be the coolest of spies and in two years tapped out more than 6,000 messages to Moscow, while finding time to maintain a wide circle of friends in Lausanne where he lived in a block of flats in Longaraie. One of his women friends wrote to the *Gazette de Lausanne* about him years later, saying 'we kidded him about being a British spy ... Someone asked him once: "In fact, what are you doing for a living?" Unperturbed, he answered: "Don't you know? I am a spy."'[6]

The role of Foote in relation to Lucas is all important because there is evidence that not only did Lucas know of Foote and his background, but that he used "Olga" as an intermediary for passing information to Foote in the hope that the latter would pass it on to the British as well as to Moscow. This came about when Lucas began to doubt whether all his messages relayed to Professor Pigou were being passed on. Wythe Williams confirmed to me long after World War II that Lucas had known all about Foote.

The "Lucy" Ring, as the set-up to which Foote belonged came to be known, was quite separate from, though occasionally linked with, the Geneva–Amsterdam network and the

INSA organization to which "Roger" belonged. "Roger" had links with London not only through Pigou, but also with that rascal, then in exile, the anti-Communist Maundy Gregory. Arthur Maundy Gregory, a former employee of MI5 in World War I, had as his "front" the proprietorship of the *Whitehall Gazette*, which had its offices in Parliament Street, Westminster. The mysterious Gregory, who spent money freely, had been shrewd enough to realize the amount of money that could be made out of the sale of honours racket which had been exploited during Lloyd George's premiership to create what became known as the Lloyd George Fund. Gregory had cashed in on this racket, but realized that there was scope for a similar racket under a Tory government. Honours were still being sold under the Tories, but more discreetly, and to nothing like the same extent as in the Lloyd George era. In 1922 a Royal Commission was set up to examine this alleged traffic and, as a direct result, legislation in the form of the Honours (Prevention of Abuses) Act, was passed to check it. Some years later Gregory was charged with having attempted to obtain £10,000 from a Lieutenant-Commander Leake in return for arranging for him to be knighted. Doubtless Gregory hoped he could bring pressure to bear to have the prosecution withdrawn by applying a little gentle blackmail on his former influential friends. This situation was summed up by J.C.C. Davidson (later Lord Davidson), the MP for Hemel Hempstead and Prime Minister Baldwin's adviser and linkman on Secret Service matters. He stated in his account of events that 'Official delight was tempered by the sober realization that he [Gregory] might reveal all in the dock.... Nobody knew to what extent Maundy Gregory would betray his past in his desperation and financial stringency. We accordingly organized someone to go to see him, who told him that he couldn't avoid a term of imprisonment, but that if he kept silent we could bring pressure to bear on the authorities to let him live in France after his sentence had been served.'[7]

As a result Gregory changed his plea of "not guilty" to one of "guilty" so that the case was dealt with by a magistrate's court and not sent to the Central Criminal Court where the penalties would have been much harsher. As a result he was sentenced to only two months' imprisonment in second division plus a fine of £50 with costs. Lord Davidson's papers, now lodged in the House of Lords, make it clear that Gregory was awarded a pension as well as being given money to live abroad. It has even been said that 'when the summons under the Honours Act was issued, he [Gregory] was offered a pension of £1,000 a year from the funds of one party, if he could plead guilty, and then go abroad and stay there, and that Gregory held out for £3,000 and got it.'[8]

But what really forced Gregory to leave the country was the fact that, quite apart from the question of the honours racket scandal, there had been demands for the exhumation of the body of Mrs Edith Rosse, who had died somewhat mysteriously while living in Gregory's home. Oddly enough, a dilatory Home Office only gave permission for the exhumation two weeks after Gregory's release from prison and his almost immediate departure for Dieppe. But some people in the Intelligence and Security Services were anxious to keep in touch with Gregory because of his extensive personal intelligence network which was as useful on Germany as it was on Russia.

'The extent of our British connections was quite astonishingly large,' states "Roger". 'We infiltrated the British Secret Service via Gregory, admittedly only to a modest degree, but it was quite useful in those frightening years 1938–41. Our contact with Gregory was through Otto Puenter and Louis Susse, a French diplomat in London, who had studied in Germany and had many contacts there. Before going into the French Foreign Service he had been a correspondent in Berlin.'[9]

Although the "Lucy" Ring has had the most publicity, in many respects the other pro-Soviet organizations in Switzerland achieved a great deal more, though in less spectacular ways. INSA (Information SA) was partly the brainchild of Pigou, and a strategy for intelligence-gathering with the minimum of risk which he strongly sponsored. This astonishing man had carried on with his mountaineering, despite having suffered fibrillation of the heart in 1925. As a sick man he had led Philip Noel-Baker and himself to safety and three days later undertook what Noel-Baker described as 'the finest climb of his career, an ascent of the face of Aiguille de la Za in icy conditions.'[10]

Pigou had been a strong anti-fascist long before Hitler came to power, directing his attacks mainly at Mussolini, and had advocated the setting-up of a Swiss-based organization both to disseminate anti-fascist news and to obtain intelligence of fascist and later of Nazi developments.

'Pigou kept very much in the background,' said "Roger", but this was roughly what INSA became when it was founded in 1928. He was ill at the time, but I remember he made a special journey to wish us well. INSA was later linked up to anti-fascist and anti-Nazi movements in Austria, Germany, Belgium and Italy. One prime reason why it was established was because Pigou was one of the first to point out that fascist-type organizations had begun to emerge in Switzerland, including a body of extremely reactionary German residents who, with their periodical, *Der Reichsdeutsche*, seemed to regard the country as an annexe of Germany.'

Otto Puenter, the chief figurehead of INSA, a native of Zurich, extended his activities to Spain during the Civil War, making a number of visits to that country for interviews with members of the international Brigade and he also founded the *Société Suisse-Espagne* for the purpose of informing the public through films, lectures and a press service of what was happening in Spain. After the promulgation of a Swiss Federal law in August 1936, forbidding any Swiss support for either side in the Civil War, the leaders of INSA all took cover names, Puenter becoming "PAKBO" (the name being comprised of the first letters of the main contact points of the organization — Pontresina, Arth-Goldau, Kreuzlingen, Berne and Orselina. Eventually the PAKBO group developed out of this at the end of the Spanish Civil War. It was, in fact, what Pigou had always advocated as a method of effective and low-key intelligence-gathering — a private "information service" which was to serve not only the Soviet Union, but all organizations which were dedicated to the overthrow of fascism. PAKBO had, at the height of its activities, contacts in Britain, France, Germany, Italy and Switzerland, as well as some thirty helpers on the frontiers — railwaymen, customs and postal employees.

PAKBO supplied information to the "Lucy" Ring, but also gave the SIS plans of the Peenemunde installations long before anyone else. Part of this information, "Roger" insists, came from Lucas directly. 'There was nobody else who could have given us such information in detail at that time.' At the same time Maundy Gregory became one of PAKBO's most valued agents and, in consequence, indirectly an agent of the USSR. Through Maundy Gregory, Louis Susse (PAKBO code-name "Salter"), obtained many details of military security measures taken by the Germans in France as well as information on various Resistance movements.

One of the key people in all this pro-Soviet activity in Switzerland was another of Pigou's early contacts with the revolutionary movement, a Slav by the name of Habijanic, whose code-name was "Max". Habijanic had been employed by the Department of Justice in the canton of Basle since about the middle of World War I. Not until the autumn of 1948 was it discovered that his side-line was the forging of Swiss passports for Soviet agents and that he had been engaged by a Swiss Communist named Franz Welti, an advocate at Basle. The most cherished member of the "Lucy" Ring was, however, "Lucy" himself and to explain his importance one cannot do better than quote from Alexander Foote: '"Lucy" could and did provide information on German aircraft and German naval shipping.... I remember that in 1941 he supplied information regarding the manufacture of flying bombs ... In effect, as far as the Kremlin were concerned, the possession of "Lucy" as a source meant that they had the equivalent of well-placed agents in the three Service Intelligence Staffs, plus the Imperial General Staff, plus the War Cabinet offices.'[11]

This may well have been an exaggeration, but it is certainly not far from the truth, considering all the sources of intelligence upon which the "Lucy" Ring could count. Foote said that when he was introduced to the network in 1941 "Lucy" made it a condition that Moscow should not be told his true identity. This made Moscow suspicious of him for quite a long time; however, as they had had good intelligence in the past from sources who insisted on remaining unknown, they persevered with him until he proved his worth. But it was the persistence of Foote, as the chief radio-operator, that enabled this intelligence to be forced on an unwilling NKVD centre in Moscow.

"Lucy" was the code-name of Rudolf Roessler, a German publisher, who moved to Switzerland after the Nazis came to power and started up a firm called *Vita Nova Verlag* in Geneva. He was eventually employed by Brigadier Masson, of the Swiss security organization, in the Bureau Ha. After the fall of France, when the Swiss were temporarily concerned about the possibility of a German invasion, his job was to assess military intelligence relating to Germany. Roessler soon proved to be a highly competent analyst of such information and also provided extremely accurate forecasts of what the Nazis would do next. But what he supplied to the Swiss he supplied in even greater detail to the Russians. His information was so vital that the Soviets eventually gave him a retainer equivalent at that time to £350 a month plus various commodity emoluments.

Roessler, however, despite having twice been convicted of spying by Swiss courts, continued long after the war to deny that he had ever indulged in espionage for any power. Many theories have been advanced as to how he had obtained such a wide range of military, naval and air intelligence for the Soviet Union. A report on the second of his trials stated: 'Roessler was one of the main wartime "contacts" of Admiral Canaris, the head of German Intelligence, and of the anti-Nazi group of officers. Though then publisher of *Nova Vita* in Lucerne, his actual function was to supply daily battle orders and other vital military intelligence to the Swiss. Without their knowledge, however, he also kept in touch with the Soviet network operating from this town and he is said to have given warning to Moscow three weeks before the German invasion.[12]

There is evidence to suggest that the Swiss and British Intelligence in Switzerland were both aware of this radio traffic long before two traitors in the Soviet network anonymously denounced Foote to the Swiss police. Yet while it is true that Brigadier Masson was privately both pro-British and pro-French and might have guessed at what was going on, the Swiss would never have risked compromising their neutrality by acquiescing in obtaining military intelligence directly from Germany by such means. On the other hand, assuming the British knew what was happening then it would have been in their interests to connive at the secret radio traffic which Foote was putting out. Stalin had been sceptical about British warnings that Germany intended to invade Russia; he had even been suspicious of similar hints from his top GRU agent, Sorge, in Tokyo. So what could have been better than for him to be brought to his senses by his own network in Switzerland?

Many of the theories about how Roessler acquired his intelligence are wide of the mark. No agent, however skilled, could have obtained such a wide range of intelligence from any single source. One such theory was that ten high-ranking Bavarian officers were jointly able to send to Roessler, by way of German radio channels, intelligence of all operations on the Eastern front. The ten Bavarians have never been named, nor has it been explained how they could achieve such a coup over so long a period.[13] Another wild theory was that Martin Bormann, Hitler's deputy, was a secret Soviet Agent. Much more feasible is the theory now generally accepted that the bulk of Roessler's material came from a variety of sources, some possibly British, and a great deal from the personal network which Lucas had set up from Germany extending into Switzerland. Certainly Lucas referred to Roessler when he spoke with Wythe Williams after the war.

10

TRAPS SET FOR RUDOLF HESS

Perhaps the most important news which Lucas was able to put through to what frequently seemed to him to be a very indifferent and ungrateful British Secret Service was that concerning Hess's interest in astrological forecasts and his grave doubts about the wisdom of carrying on a war against the British. Lucas could see the advantages the British might gain through such information, while at the same time he feared that this might give encouragement to the still moderately powerful appeasement party within the government.

From FBI sources it is clear that the British SIS were noncommittal about Lucas. They do not seem to have said anything against him, but they were always seeking information on him. If they knew he had contacts inside both the German and Russian hierarchy, then perhaps they had reason to be cautious, but they might at least have realized that this could give them an advantage they had never had before. Lucas suspected, rightly as it turned out, that he had an enemy either in Scotland Yard or MI5, and he was puzzled why this should be. He also suspected that MI5 might have passed information on him to the SIS.

'The fact that I had a British mother did not seem to count for anything,' Lucas ruefully told one British member of SIS then stationed in Switzerland. 'Sorry,' was the reply, 'but I suggest you try Naval Intelligence. They will always listen.'

Lucas was given the name of a contact in British Naval Intelligence, but, being always on the move in and out of various countries at this time, he had to rely on an intermediary. Whether this was ''Olga'' I do not know, but the message did get through to the Naval Intelligence Division where it was taken seriously by Ian Fleming, then personal assistant to the Director of the Service. Fleming had spent some time in Switzerland as a young man and had many contacts in that country. Years later, when he was foreign manager of Kemsley Newspapers, and I was on his staff, he told me that, 'nobody else would listen about Hess and astrology. Even our people were doubtful, but I kept on pushing them. In the end it was suggested that NID couldn't do much, but someone else might, and I decided to be the someone else who might effectively exploit this idea.' Fleming asked me not to breathe a word of this story while he was alive, and it was not until six years after his death that I told in my *History of the British Secret Service* how: 'Fleming had studied the dossier on Admiral Sir Barry Domville, the pro-German Director of Naval Intelligence of 1927–30, and this had led him to examine, first of all out of idle curiosity, the history of The Link [this was the Anglo–German society which came into existence after Hitler's coming to power]. He had also had a keen insight into the psychological make-up of the German character and of the preoccupation of top-ranking Nazis with astrology and the occult. As a result of this he thought up the idea of recreating The Link and building up a fictitious picture of how it had gone underground and acquired new and even more influential members who could pave the way to a negotiated peace with Germany and the overthrow of the Churchill Government. If this kind of information could be leaked to some gullible Nazi leader, then he believed that not only might Germany's invasion plans be shelved, but that Nazis could be misled into secretly sending some important figure in their hierarchy to Britain.'[1]

Fleming knew that such an extravaganza of Secret Service technique would be unlikely to commend itself to the NID and that the project would raise all kinds of political objections, but he did try to interest the NID, both on this occasion and again much later. This is clearly shown by Fleming's own investigations, and by the many references to the involvement of Intelligence in horoscopy and necromancy which appear in the memoirs of Admiral Sir John Godfrey (DNI 1940–41), stored in the archives of Churchill College, Cambridge.[2]

Feeling that speed of action was needed, Fleming quickly

decided to by-pass his own NID and push his project in other quarters. He felt it was far too hazardous to handle on his own, but, reluctant to let go of a scheme which appealed to his imaginative mind, he passed the idea to two trusted friends, one who was in another branch of British Intelligence, the other a contact in Switzerland who was an authority on astrology.

Fleming's Swiss contact succeeded in planting on Rudolf Hess an astrologer who was also a British agent. One can easily imagine Fleming, tongue-in-cheek, briefing the astrologer for the task in hand, allowing his imagination full play and painting a convincing picture of aristocratic plotters waiting in British country houses for the signal from a Nazi leader to bring about the downfall of the Churchill Government. Fleming's methods of work were frequently circumlocutory and, where and when he saw fit, deliberately obscure. He had the uncanny skill when briefing people of giving less than the information required, thus completely disguising the purpose of an operation while cajoling some mystified subordinate into doing the right thing without his knowing why he was doing it.

It was essential that the theme of the plot should be worked into a conventional horoscope so the Swiss contact obtained two horoscopes from astrologers who were known to Hess personally to enable the British agent to produce one that was not suspiciously different yet was capable of luring Hess into his flight to Britain on a highly improbable mission. At the same time, again based to some extent on information from Lucas, the recreation of The Link was developed to fit in with the horoscope forecast. Towards the end of 1940, agents in the Café Chiada in Lisbon and in another café in Berne were slowly but surely shaping events which led to one of the most dramatic incidents of the war.

Lucas had discovered that Hess had his own private intelligence service quite apart from the *Verbindungsstab*. His informant here was a young secretary called Helga Stultz, working in the archives of the Berghof, who was an informer for the American Intelligence at a later stage of the war. It seems almost certain that Helga's other cover names were "Clara" and "Olga". The details of her life — right down to the secret marriage to an aide of Captain Roehm, who was purged in the blood bath of June 30 1934 — tally exactly with Lucas's own many published comments on "Clara", even though the information on Helga was obtained quite independently of Lucas.

Helga Stultz passed intelligence to the Americans via Switzerland, including a report transferred to Washington before the outbreak of World War II of a conversation between Hitler and Dr Robert Ley, a close friend of the American businessman Charles Eugene Bedaux, who was a member of the Windsors' intimate circle, to the effect that 'Lloyd George's position is not easy. He has to pretend to work with the left-wing of his own Party and the ruling clique mistrust him. But I am not without hope that Lothian [the Marquis of Lothian, British Ambassador to the USA] may play a part in removing the ruling clique's dislike of L1.G.'

For a long time nobody in the US government paid much heed to this, but meanwhile Lucas himself was probing into the membership of the *Verbindungsstab* and their connections either with the original organization known as The Link, or with the bogus Link which was to be used as a trap for Hess and his allies. Volume X of the *Documents on German Foreign Policy* shows that Ribbentrop and the German Foreign Office were convinced, after the fall of France, that they could induce the Duke of Windsor — then in Madrid and Lisbon — to stay on in Europe instead of leaving to become Governor of the Bahamas. They were certain that he would lend himself to their peace campaign and that he and Lloyd George could be brought into secret accord. Their efforts in this direction range from the sinister to the fatuous and, as the book rightly states, 'the German records are necessarily a tainted source. The only firm evidence they provide is of what the Germans were trying to do in this matter and how completely they failed to do it.'

An elaborate plot to kidnap the Duke and Duchess was ordered by Hitler and Ribbentrop, and the man chosen to organize it was Walter Schellenberg, the Intelligence chief. It was to have been implemented while the Duke was hunting near the Spanish frontier; he was to have been lured across by a ruse and taken to the German Embassy in Madrid. At the last moment, however, the British had warning of the plot, the Duke cancelled his shooting trip and guards were posted around the villa where he was staying just outside Lisbon.

Schellenberg, who went to Madrid to organize this ambitious coup, wrote in his journal: 'I had accomplices in the house where the Duke was staying. Servants at table were in my pay and reported to me all that was said.'[3]

Helga Stultz provided further enlightenment on this peace campaign in a report to Washington: 'Hitler has been in a terrible mood. I am sure he will repudiate the German–Soviet Pact. Ribbentrop is most anxious not to upset the Russians, but I do not think his view will prevail. Hess sides with Hitler; he believed that Germany must settle her account with Russia and that by doing this some agreement can be reached with England. Hess is so confident of this that I feel sure he has had imported news from England ... Hess is contemptuous of the *Abwehr* and is pursuing his own ideas of espionage. He has organized the *Verbindungsstab*, which is so far the only real attempt to build a co-ordinated espionage system. It is interesting that the Welsh section of *Verbindungsstab* has been set up in Lisbon. The Café Chiado in the Rua Garetta in Lisbon is a rendezvous for their meetings. The Hotel Riff in Tangier is another.'[4]

Clearly Lucas too had been put fully in the picture regarding Hess's secret schemes, for in a letter which "Clara" ("Helga" "Olga") wrote to him she stated: 'Last night Rudolph Hess had a long conference with Hitler in the latter's study. Hess returned from a trip to Madrid only a few days ago. He travelled incognito and no one here had the faintest idea of what it all meant. The first clue I obtained of these doings was through Hess's talk with Hitler. Hess went to Spain on his own initiative ... He went to Madrid for the purpose of reaching Sir Samuel Hoare, British Ambassador ... While he had discussed the project with no one, not even Hitler, the Gestapo apparently had gotten wind of it. Anyway, Hess has complained to Hitler that Himmler was dispatched to Madrid hurriedly so that the Gestapo chief could spy on Hess. Hess said he would have remained in Madrid if Himmler had not urged him to return to Germany. While in Madrid, Hess did not see Sir Samuel Hoare, but he contrived to reach the British through friendly Spanish sources — Hess gained the impression that his suggestions might meet with consideration if he could get them to the direct attention of certain circles in

England. He mentioned several names to Hitler, but pronounced them so hurriedly that I could not get them.

'Now, this is what Hess proposes to do. He wants to fly to England alone. This undertaking in itself, he contends, would be so spectacular that the warmongers now directing British policy could not keep it a secret.'[5]

Unfortunately, there was a long delay in this vital piece of information getting through to Wythe Williams. It was not until after the news broke that Rudolph Hess had landed in Scotland and been taken prisoner that "Linda" reported that "Clara" had not informed her soon enough about the talk between Hess and Hitler as "Clara" had almost immediately gone back into Switzerland on hearing the news. "Linda" and her close colleague Wolfgang decided that Lucas must be told, but the detailed explanatory letter about the whole affair was delayed in transit and did not reach Wythe Williams for some time. The basis for an article on the Hess affair, which was published not in *Greenwich Time* (it was felt this was too risky from a security viewpoint), but in *Liberty Magazine*, was a secret radio message from the tiny neutral state of Liechtenstein.[6]

Alas, the decision to go into print was an error. For obvious reasons the radio message was guarded, even though it was in code and, as the letter which eventually arrived from "Linda" made clear, the radio message was an inadequate basis for an article. Its essence was that "red was the colour", meaning that an invasion of Russia was a certainty, but where Wythe Williams erred, in order to give substance and authority to his article in *Liberty Magazine*, was in revealing part of the code text and in stating that it was sent from Vaduz, the capital of Liechtenstein. When Lucas learned about this he was furious. He felt it could easily lead to the detection of his contact in Vaduz by the Gestapo. To make matters worse it turned out that the message had been filed not by the contact in Vaduz but by Wolfgang, an ally of "Clara", who could easily be traced back by his close links to Ribbentrop. Naturally, German Intelligence, keeping a close watch on what appeared in American journals, would note the code reference and also the fact that the item appeared in *Liberty Magazine* only three days before the Germans invaded the USSR.

Wolfgang had probably been the bravest and keenest member of Lucas's private network, prepared to take more risks than most. What he did not know was that he was already under Gestapo surveillance. Lucas, always a realist, had constantly advised Wolfgang to join the Gestapo, realizing that not only did some of the best intelligence come from this quarter, but also that membership was a safeguard for a double-agent. Wolfgang, however, so detested the organization that he would not agree to Lucas's suggestion. Shortly after he returned to Germany he was watched even more carefully and his contacts with "Clara" were noted. As a result he was caught copying out secret documents and challenged as he left the grounds of Fuschl Castle. Being armed, he tried to shoot his way out of trouble, but was himself shot down and killed.

Meanwhile, Hess was in prison in Britain and even Dr Goebbels' propaganda machine did not try to disguise the role played by astrology. (One of the astrologers consulted by Hess was Karl Ernest Krafft and this association is confirmed in some considerable detail by various sources.[7]) In May 1941 an article appeared in the German press which stated that 'as was well known in Party circles, Rudolph Hess was in poor health for many years and latterly increasingly had recourse to hypnotists, astrologers and so on. The extent to which these people are responsible for the mental confusion which led him to his present step has still to be clarified.[8] As a result of this the Germans launched what was known as the *Aktion Hess* which led to the arrest of hundreds of people, with astrologers at the top of the list.

The question is, who was the astrologer planted on Hess by Ian Fleming? "Roger" says the code-name was "Vanessa", and that she was to assure Hess that he could count on every support from certain people within the United Kingdom 'Hess was infatuated with "Vanessa", but much more with her mind and opinions than in any other sense. We understood that "Vanessa" might have been part Irish and part British, but no more than that. My own part in this was to help to publicise "Vanessa" as being hostile to Britain on account of Ireland and that she was eager to do all she could to ensure total control by Eire over Northern Ireland.'

One might assume that "Vanessa's" astrological chart

deliberately concocted to lure Hess to Britain despite all orthodox predictions by the other allegedly reputable astrologers of the day. A careful analysis of these astrologers' predictions has been made by Nicholas Campion, of Queen's College, Cambridge, one of the founders of the Institute for the Study of Cycles in World Affairs, formed in 1980, which set out to investigate astrology. Mr Campion writes: 'in view of your opinion that the astrological advice was "cooked up" by British Intelligence, I cast the horoscope for the time at which Hess took off for Britain. The horoscope for this time is most inauspicious. I have since had the chart looked at by somebody who is more familiar with certain traditional rules than I. It transpires that this is a most evil horoscope in any traditional sense, largely because six planets are in the house of death and two other points are strong: the fixed star Algol (which leads one to lose one's head) and the evil degree Serpentis (the accursed degree of the accursed sign). It follows that if Hess picked the time of his flight from orthodox astrological advice, then the astrologers advising him were well aware they were picking a time which they saw as ensuring failure. It also seems that they were picking a chart which, from the astrological point of view, predicts not only failure but death.'[9]

"Roger" thought that Ian Fleming might have checked up with Aleister Crowley, another student of the occult, when "Vanessa's" name was submitted to him. Not even Churchill could be sure of all the Secret Service manoeuvres regarding the Hess affair — he certainly did not know about the unofficial scheme which Fleming had hatched — contrary to general belief, Secret Services quite wisely do not always tell their governments what they do.

Fleming undoubtedly felt that a great chance of propaganda victory had been lost, but the inhibitions which prevented the Government from fully exploiting Hess's arrival were due to the fear that the pro-German influence in high places was still strong. No one wanted to invite a propaganda counter-attack about the existence of a pro-German movement in Britain.

One of Fleming's more whimsical ideas was that Aleister Crowley should be sent to interview Hess in captivity. Crowley was, of course, a notorious necromancer, but he had been an informant on intelligence matters over many years. No doubt

Fleming's idea was that Crowley could have pursued with Hess all manner of astrological queries and discovered more about the influence of astrologers on other Nazi leaders. But the requested interview never took place.

The story of this master-plot set up by a few individualists working on their own has been carefully guarded over the years, possibly because it concerns important people in the background, in particular some of those close to the mysterious "Vanessa". It is a story which has been denied by some, but German astrologers were convinced of its authenticity and Kapitan zur See Alfred Wolff, who had been flag officer to Admiral Doenitz, was insistent that Hess's defection had been schemed by the British.

Another angle on this is provided by one of the more unusual messages which came from the Lucas network to *Greenwich Time* in the early part of 1940; a plea for Wythe Williams to locate Bela Kiss, the Hungarian astrologer who had become a mass-murderer in the early part of the century.

Kiss had discovered his wife with a lover, garrotted them and hidden their bodies in empty petrol drums. Telling his neighbours that his wife and her lover had run away, he began to receive female visitors week after week at his home. When war came in 1914 he was conscripted and, after he had left for the front, a collection of petrol drums was found at his home, opened and discovered to contain the corpses of several naked women preserved in alcohol, as well as those of his wife and her lover.

It transpired that Kiss had advertised (under another name) for female companions and had persuaded the women who responded to the advertisements to part with their savings before he murdered them.

Kiss was supposedly killed in action, but in fact he had simply exchanged his identity with that of another soldier killed on the battlefield. After the war he was reported to have joined the French Foreign Legion, but by the time the Hungarian police had picked up his trail he had deserted. Word was that he had gone to New York and that he was working for the Nazis as an astrologer-agent, putting over the kind of forecasts which the Germans wanted the American public to read.

Kiss was never traced, but the interesting part of this story is that it shows how Hess may not only have been misled by "Vanessa" and other astrologers who fed him faked horoscopes, but also by the Nazi propagandist astrologers who were doing much the same thing, though for a different purpose.

The puzzle remains: what was the real identity of "Vanessa"? The Hess Papers on the British side are still not declassified, or available for inspection. No adequate reason has been given for this, despite the fact that Hess arrived in Britain forty-eight years ago on his daring flight from Germany and the normal time limit in Britain for de-classification is thirty years, and despite the fact that Hess is now dead.

It is said that there are also some papers concerning Hess in the Royal Archives at Windsor, which might contain letters he sent to King George VI. However, this may well be a confusion of Rudolph Hess with the Prince of Hesse, a leading Nazi and a relative of Prince Philip, Princesse Marina and other members of the Royal Family. (It was to rescue incriminating papers from the Hesse family home that Anthony Blunt was sent to Germany on a secret mission for the Royal family at the end of the war: the Hesse residence was in the American Zone of Germany and there was some concern that information on the papers might get into the hands of the US media.)

There are two possible candidates for the identity of "Vanessa", both still alive. In 1987, shortly after Hess's death, there appeared in the French newspaper, *Le Monde*, an article entitled *Digressions* by one Bernard Frank which points to one of them. He wrote: 'I wonder what Vanessa O'Shaughnessy, third daughter of Brian and Helene, would have thought of the death of Rudolph Hess by suicide. After all, if Hess parachuted into Scotland, one day in May 1941, it was because of his love for Vanessa, and it was because of her that he remained in prison for more than forty-six years. One remembers that having observed a form of retreat, Vanessa took the veil ... There, where she is, she is probably ignorant of the death of her lover. She was tall and blonde with horse-like features. My impression is that the international press should have interrogated Jean d'Ormesson, after all, Jean d'Ormesson is without doubt *the man in France* who knew best Rudolph.'[10]

Jean d'Ormesson is a distinguished and highly respected member of the French Academy and he has written three books in which Rudolph Hess is mentioned — *Le Vent du Soir, Tous les hommes en sont fous* and *Le Bonheur à San Miniato*. In his last book the reader discovers that Hess went on his mission to England because of his love for 'Vanessa O'Shaughnessy' [sic]. When I wrote to M. d'Ormesson for some enlightenment on this story, he replied cordially but insisted that his story was fiction.[11]

Now it is not unusual for fictional works to be created around real people, but normally (if only to make them seem realistic and intriguing) some hitherto unknown facts are introduced to make such stories credible. One would expect a French academician to act likewise, even if he disguised the facts. So the question remains: are there facts behind the fiction, and why the coincidence of the name of "Vanessa" which was known to "Roger" back in the late 1930's, if not the early 1940's?

"Roger" claims that Lucas's most urgent messages to the British were to warn them of an attractive, but highly dangerous peace offer from Germany. '"Werther", as we knew him, insisted it was a trap and that the Nazis had no intention of keeping their part of any such bargain once they had dealt with the Russians. The aim was to get through to King George VI a letter from Hess which contained a peace proposal. This was that if Britain agreed to a peace settlement, allowing Hitler to concentrate on an attack on the USSR, Hitler would guarantee not merely the survival of Britain as an independent state, but of the British Empire as well.'

The major query still is whether Hess gave the British vital information on Germany's plans to launch an invasion of Russia, which occurred only two weeks later. Stalin always believed that Hess did so and that the warning was not passed on to him. If, as the late Sir Maurice Oldfield (head of MI6) maintained, the Russians had infiltrated Hess's private intelligence, then it is possible that they could have learned about the invasion plan this way and realized that Churchill had withheld vital information from them. (Not that there was any legitimate reason at that time why Churchill or any other Briton should have passed intelligence to a nation which had a pact with Germany.)

The truth as Lucas knew full well from his contacts with

both Russians and Germans is that at that time, while Churchill was regarded as the right man in the right job by the vast mass of the British people, he was still surrounded by, and being plotted against by, a wide range of appeasers of varying strengths from politicians to some inside the Royal circle. This was why Lucas regarded it as essential that Hess should be lured to Britain, caught and imprisoned, rather than allowed to conduct his peace offers through overseas and neutral channels where they might have done more damage.

It has always been regarded as highly uncivilized and unjust that Hess should have been kept in Spandau Prison all those years until his death. The official British reason for supporting this plan (even during the periods when they were in charge of Spandau) has always been that the Russians would not allow Hess to be released. Yet in the one year in which the USSR failed to make a formal objection to his release, the British themselves registered one. Could the reason have been that the British needed to suppress documented evidence that Hess had been encouraged to come to Britain by highly placed sympathisers in this country?

11

LUCAS SCORES MORE SCOOPS

The ingenuity of Lucas's communications was quite remarkable. His resourcefulness in getting messages through to Wythe Williams whether by radio, cables, letters or postcards from places remote from the scene of war was unending. It was in January 1940, that Williams began his regular series of radio commentaries on the progress of the war, using Lucas's material to make a few prophecies. Towards the end of February 1940, he said: 'Everyone is discussing the Western Front and the Balkans, but there is a spot on the map called Denmark. Advices reaching me indicate that Hitler is concentrating a considerable force along the Danish border. This should mean that Denmark will be his first objective.'[1]

Lucas managed to pick up news of his friends' broadcast and on one of his forays into Switzerland sent this cable to Williams' private address: 'Greetings. Dolphi will make excursion to Alsen just as Otto did.' Williams himself stated shortly afterwards that this cable came from 'a Scandinavian port', but this was a cover-up for the actual place which was Lausanne. By now the two men were attuned to each other's thoughts sufficiently for Williams to spot the clues in Lucas's coded language. "Dolphi" meant Hitler, as Lucas had told Williams that this was the pet name which Eva Braun, Hitler's companion, had given the Fuhrer. But Williams had to do some research on the other references in the cable. Alsen he located as a small island off the Danish coast. Then, by referring to various encyclopaedias, he discovered that in 1864, when Prince Otto von Bismarck was Chancellor of Prussia, he had sent in troops to take over Alsen. On 9 April 1940 Hitler duly ordered the German army to take over Denmark while he invaded Norway.

Shortly after this Lucas once again arrived in America. As a result of picking up information from Karin Hall, Berchtesgaden and all his contacts there, he warned that the fall of France was imminent. Realizing that few in the USA had any indication of the true nature of Germany's military superiority (most Americans had a vague idea that the Maginot Line was impregnable), he produced copies of confidential reports showing how Hitler had 12,000 combat planes compared with France's 2,000 (of inferior quality), while the Germans also had nearly 1,700 dive bombers against a minimal total for the French. 'France has men mobilized,' said Lucas, 'and four million such would appear to suggest a hell of a lot of divisions, maybe over two hundred. But the truth is that the divisions lack weapons, and the true total of actually armed divisions is no more than about half this size.'

Even Williams, the experienced former foreign correspondent, was half inclined to think Lucas was exaggerating. He, like the rest, had the idea that the Maginot Line was still a massive deterrent. 'Not in Berchtesgaden,' replied Lucas. 'They are fully aware of all the ways around it.'

The way around it was, as Lucas gathered, the very point where the Maginot Line ended in the area of Sedan. Therefore, Lucas argued, disaster lay ahead very soon — the defeat of France with Britain left entirely alone. Communications between himself and New York became much more of a problem as there was a curiously ambivalent attitude inside the Roosevelt administration on the subject of the war. 'Roosevelt wants another term of office for himself more than anything else,' said Lucas. 'He is the concealed egoist, revelling in power but with very little idea of how to exploit it. Only the harsh facts of life will bring him back to reality. There are still ditherers inside his administration and especially in the diplomatic service. In that field America has a lot to learn. Roosevelt, for all his charisma, is what we call in Russia an onanistic do-gooder. Not quite the right translation, but something close to it. He spills his goodwill around like a prize masturbator.'

If I am putting these words into Lucas's mouth in those early months of 1940, I can only justify this by adding that, except of course for the references to another term of office for Roosevelt, that is exactly what he said in my presence in 1942. It rather shocked me at the time when we British tended to see the US President through rose-tinted spectacles, but gradually history proved Lucas right as the errors of FDR's administration became plainer to see.

It was because of his fears about Roosevelt in the long term that Lucas was insistent that the USA must be woken up to the facts of life, and as in 1940 events were moving fast he decided communications must be speeded up. Also, Lucas still had to convince Williams that he really was getting first-class, top priority intelligence and I am sure that his plan of setting up a special receiver set was partly to convince Williams that somehow he was getting German military orders direct from the Reich. Certainly Lucas had need for a special receiving set, but for rather more mundane purposes than he suggested, such as listening in to a wide range of foreign broadcasts and perhaps occasionally picking up an unexpected gem of information which he was not supposed to hear.

At this time Lucas's network, both inside and outside Germany, was running considerable risks. To keep this network in existence was in itself a major task, but if it was not to disintegrate, it had to remain undetected. That meant ensuring that clandestine communications left no trace. He had gained enormous experience in studying such systems used by the various networks in Switzerland and elsewhere. One of his closest advisers had been a British operator in Switzerland who believed Lucas was working on the Soviet side. This man was a member of the Soviet network.

Frequent denials have been made that any clandestine radio could have operated between Europe and the USA in this period without either detection or connivance, as all wavelengths were monitored. Apart from this, whatever the experts might have claimed, transmission at vast distances was still not easy. Much of the clandestine radio network depended upon communications between adjacent territories and other means of passing on information from there. "Roger" reported that a young Dutchman who had been a member of the communist underground in Holland and who had briefly been imprisoned in Germany for pro-communist activities, had been 'chosen to establish a clandestine radio station in Britain and another, if possible, in Ireland. So much vital intelligence was already being obtained from Britain at this time that it was considered necessary to have this re-transmitted direct in the event of war. Cambridge was chosen as a centre because we had contacts there.'[2]

The truth is that Lucas relied on others to pick up much of his direct intelligence from Germany, and sometimes it was wiser to pretend that he had himself collected this from German military radio than to compromise others. Where he seems to have scored heavily was in gaining access to German codes. Even an amateur, using a transmitter-receiver apparatus of only 10 watts output, could operate undetected with a reasonable amount of luck, provided he moved his set from one area to another within a given perimeter, kept the periods of transmission very short, and varied his times of operating. The British, and especially the Bletchley organization engaged in deciphering, maintained ridiculous claims that they and they alone were effective and nobody else could touch them. This is nonsense: David Kahn, an acknowledged expert on code-breaking, states that 'by 1942 they [the Russians] had cracked messages in the Enigma [i.e. the German messages].'[3]

Those who worked in the Bletchley team rather tend to doubt this assertion, though they admit it is possible. But both Constantine Fitzgibbon and Group-Captain F.W. Winter-botham seem to agree that the Russians received much material either via the "Lucy" Ring, or direct from American and British sources. Group-Captain Winterbotham has, however, told the author: 'I am certain the USSR had very useful agents in the German HQ.'

This evidence by acknowledged specialists in this field should also be weighed against "Roger's" information. "Roger" was extremely active in this whole field of communications, having a cover that was never "blown", and serving the Russians through channels which he will still not specify. He has long since ceased any such activities, but while critical of the USSR, wishes to remain neutral. He claims that through Lucas's contacts with Britain, and with Professor Pigou in particular, 'a Soviet transmission centre in Cambridge was set up shortly before the war. It was largely controlled by Dutch

Communist agents working independently of, but guided and advised on problems of locations by Pigou, who knew the terrain intimately. Sometimes the transmitter was moved out as far as Duxford, Trumpington or even Great Shelford, but at others it was in the heart of Cambridge. This is how the Soviet transmission set-up in Cambridge was able to operate sporadically during the war. They must have used at least twenty different locations. But I would stress this was not an official Soviet link, but merely intended as an aid to Soviet intelligence. It had nothing whatsoever to do with Ruth Kuchinsky [Kucynzski], or "Lucy". Transmission to Cambridge was confined to very occasional short messages, mainly consisting of a series of five digit numbers delivered by voice transmission. The Soviets, of course, maintained their own radio link with Moscow for the duration of the war, and they were able to do this partly through information on technical developments from Britain, not least those concerning the detection of radio messages.'

At this time, however, Lucas's main concern was to find out what the Germans were planning in the United States and to try to obtain any codes they were using. Most of this information came from either his contacts in Karin Hall or Berchtesgaden, or from Switzerland. At this time it was of the utmost importance for him to be able to tell Wythe Williams exactly what the Gestapo links were within the USA. What the *Greenwich Time* editor desperately needed was information on Nazi or Gestapo activities on American soil so that he could show the Germans in a bad light. Williams was increasingly and totally unjustifiably being accused of being pro-Nazi because he kept reporting the gains the Germans were making, about which the rest of the world was not being told, and also the future gains they seemed likely to make. To some readers and radio listeners this sounded like pro-German propaganda.

Lucas's plan was to keep his ears open for news of all German officials being sent out to the USA. Eventually he thought that he had detected the man who had been nominated as the new senior Gestapo observer in the USA and he decided to get himself booked as a passenger aboard the ship in which this man, code-named "Gerda", was travelling. During the voyage Lucas had several chats with "Gerda", making it clear that they had mutual friends at Berchestgaden. He soon discovered that "Gerda" had the reputation of being one of the ablest and cleverest of Gestapo agents, who had been given the post of managing director of a respectable chemical firm as cover for his American trip. Further, he learned the names of some of the people "Gerda" would contact within the German community in the USA.

Exactly what happened in the case of "Gerda" is uncertain. One theory was that "Gerda" had made himself enemies inside the Gestapo because some of his colleagues had learned that he had been secretly spying on some of their rackets, on the orders of the Gestapo chief, Himmler. As a result there was a plot to liquidate him, either by a planned killing, or by allowing information about him to be passed to the British so that he would be detained en route when the ship called at an inspection port. Lucas's own story was that "Gerda" (who he referred to as "Friedrich Homburg") was taken away by an inspection team when 'we were pulling into Kirkwall, the British inspection port in the Orkneys . . . I saw him and his baggage taken ashore and I never saw him again.'

However, this story seems highly improbable on several counts and is almost certainly a cover-up. It is highly unlikely that the Germans would allow any of their officials to run the risk of passing through a British port. Also, if Lucas's story were true in every detail, its publication would have made it easy for the German Intelligence to make certain deductions which would have led to the unmasking not only of Lucas himself, but of at least two of his Gestapo contacts inside Berchtesgaden. Even if Lucas himself had by that time decided it was unsafe to return to Germany, he was far too careful and loyal a character to risk the lives of any in his network.

Nonetheless it would seem that the information which Lucas gained on "Gerda" was ultimately of great value to the American authorities, who began to see how the Nazis were stepping up their campaign inside the USA, and it led to an attempt by him to infiltrate the New York branch of the Gestapo, a branch much more efficient and dangerous than their Washington undercover counterpart. What was more this led Lucas into a meeting with Captain Fritz Wiedemann, once Hitler's company commander in World War I, and now

Consul-General in San Francisco. But Wiedemann, a wily intriguer and negotiator, moved around in America quite frequently and their meeting took place in New York.

Wythe Williams maintained his reputation as an accurate prophet of what was happening in Europe in his newspaper articles and radio broadcasts. On 13 May 1940, he was able to warn that 'unless General Gamelin makes a complete change in his plans, the Allied armies are facing terrible danger. Hitler has laid an ingenious trap for them. If they withdraw from Belgium in haste and take up defensive positions behind the Maginot Extension, they may stand a chance of holding off the German onslaught. But if they throw all their available field strength into Belgium and offer battle on the plains of Flanders, strong German armoured forces will break through the Meuse River Gap at Sedan, flank the Maginot Extension from the east and continue to the sea where they will cut off the Allied retreat.'[4]

This broadcast more than any other caused poor Williams much misery: again he was accused of being pro-Nazi and violently attacked for being an irresponsible alarmist. But within days what he had predicted, on the basis of Lucas's assessments, was proved correct. The French Ninth Army on the Sedan front was defeated by the Germans, and, shortly afterwards, a German *panzer* division, commanded by the then Lieutenant-General (later Field-Marshal) Erwin Rommel, arrived at the Channel coast off Abbeville and cut off the Allied armies.

Next Lucas received a tip from Wolfgang, allegedly written in Russian. One wonders whether this was not a Russian rather than a German report, cleverly attributed to Wolfgang. It indicated that Mussolini was about to declare war against Britain largely on the excuse that he did not really trust Hitler and wanted to have a say in any peace conference. Williams broadcast on 7 June 1940, that 'Mussolini is about to throw Italy into the fray at any moment.' Three days later this was exactly what happened.

At this time there came a hint of some kind of financial assistance for Lucas in maintaining his network. He received a cable in New York which read: 'Eugen suffered a stroke and passed away. His will establishes you as chief beneficiary of his estate. This may prove a satisfactory solution of your financial obligation.' The explanation for this somewhat mysterious cable was that Lucas had undertaken to set up a fund in Switzerland upon which any member of his network could draw if and when forced to escape from Germany. The cable suggests that Eugen had in some way made plans to add to this fund.

Up to this moment, though Lucas himself said little about it, financial support was the biggest problem the network had. It would have seemed impossible to the outside world that a mini-intelligence service, controlled by one man, should produce such instant, accurate information without substantial funds. It frequently seemed impossible even to Wythe Williams, but every time he had doubts the Lucas prophecies were substantiated.

By the summer of 1940 almost everything depended upon what Lucas gained from the network, as he himself was then more or less permanently in New York. "Linda" supplied him with facts and figures on German aircraft production so that Williams was able to broadcast in August 1940, that he was 'in possession today of an interesting report on the subject of changes in present and potential air strength of the two sides in the conflict ... According to the same confidential source which gave me the correct figures at the end of May, the number of newly-manufactured aircraft turned over by German planes to the air command of Hermann Goering totalled 3,820, which is 140 planes below the record May figure. Of these 420 were long-range bombers, 880 dive-bombers, 560 pursuit planes, 740 combat planes, 290 combination combat and bombing planes and 660 military transport planes. The remaining 270 planes were for auxiliary services. The disproportionately large number of newly-constructed dive-bombers is highly significant, considering the impending air blitz against England.'[5]

By this time British observers in the USA, especially those attached to British Intelligence, were becoming increasingly curious about and envious of the information Wythe Williams was obtaining. So, for that matter, were the American military officials who feared that some of these planes might find their way to Japan. Reports from Germany and Switzerland from members of the network suggested that, though they could still produce a great deal of news of German plans in relation to Britain, France and Italy, each day the risks became greater. Much depended upon what Klaus Mann would be able to achieve on one of his visits.

While Lucas was absolutely satisfied that Mann was not a double-agent, he felt sure that as long as America remained a neutral nation he had Germany's full approval of his trips backwards and forwards across the Atlantic. The obtaining of dollars seemed to be the clue to this, no more and no less. However, Lucas began to suspect that Klaus Mann might also be secretly passing on some intelligence to the Americans; he observed that the 'US State Department always released information on secret Nazi designs soon after Mann's return from one of his mysterious trips.' During one of these trips the versatile Klaus Mann dealt with the matter of Lucas's inheritance from Eugen, somehow very neatly managing to turn it into cash amounting to the equivalent of some twelve thousand dollars. Half of this sum he switched to Switzerland so that it could be drawn from in emergencies by any in the network who needed it. As to the other half, Mann's story was that it had cost him this much in bribes to make all the arrangements. Williams told Lucas that he thought this was somewhat outrageous behaviour and that Mann must have made quite a lot for himself. Surprisingly, Lucas did not seem so concerned. 'I have long since learned not to worry too much about money,' he replied, 'and in any case Klaus worked a miracle in wartime. The others are safe, that's what matters most.'

From about this period most of the network's letters were sent to the United States via various centres in Latin America and, consequently, they often arrived very late. Then came news that "Linda" had been arrested for spying. Apparently she had taken a copy of the Military Convention between Germany and Japan which she obtained at Karin Hall, and the military security police had discovered this. For two days she was kept under arrest, and then, with a colleague's help, she got herself out of trouble by saying that the copy she had was to have been sent to Hitler on his instructions. Nobody dared check this detail with Hitler, so "Linda" was released.

Gradually the network decreased after, first, Wolfgang's

death, and then Linda's surprise marriage to a German who was shortly afterwards posted to a neutral country. Thus the main figures left of the original team were Clara in Switzerland, where as "Olga" she built up other contacts, and the two members of the Gestapo who continued to risk their lives in the cause of freedom.

12

"OLGA" GIVES NEWS ON JAPAN

From late 1940 until the United States came into the war some sections of American intelligence and counter-intelligence began to pay considerable attention to Lucas. It is not clear whether he allowed his name to be put forward to these services, or whether he tried to make his own contacts with them. But links were certainly established long before it was decided to create the Office of Strategic Services under General William J. Donovan at the outbreak of war against Japan.

Lucas was well aware of the imperfections of American Intelligence generally, especially as the nation lacked any realistic form of secret service in the late 1930's. Ideally, he should have been recruited into the OSS, which, despite many criticisms, gradually grew into quite a formidable and aggressive organization. But from all accounts this path forward was barred to him for various reasons, not the least of which was that the FBI took a close interest in watching, if not actually controlling him. They had learned that Lucas had many contacts in Latin America, and even after the OSS was set up under Roosevelt's personal orders, it was decreed that Nelson Rockefeller and J. Edgar Hoover of the FBI were to operate in Latin America. The OSS was absolutely forbidden to operate within and from Mexico and places south, a major handicap to the new service.

It was about this time that Lucas began to drop hints of German plans for extending the influence of the Nazi Party in Latin America, especially through links with fascist parties in Argentina, Paraguay, Brazil and Peru. At the same time he warned of increasing ties with Japan, some of which were

linked to Latin American states. The latter warnings were
never given the prominence they deserved either in the press or
radio reports, or elsewhere. Above all, Lucas said, Japan
wanted ready access to all sources of oil. He also argued that
Roosevelt, by goading the Japanese in foolish ways, had paved
the way towards a Japanese–German outright alliance at a
very delicate stage.

In August 1942, Roosevelt brought in a series of economic
sanctions against Japan, which included an oil embargo. His
naval and military advisers had tried to dissuade him from this
course, and Prince Konoye had almost begged to see Roosevelt
alone to thrash out these problems, but Roosevelt went ahead.
The inevitable result, as Lucas again indicated, was the military dictatorship of General Togo. Stalin, of course, wished to
see Japan involved in the war, and it was the influence of the
pro-Communists in circles close to the President who helped
ensure this would happen — men like Lauchlin Currie, Nathan
Silvermaster and Michael Greenberg. Even Oliver Lyttelton,
Production Minister in Churchill's War Cabinet, told the
American Chamber of Commerce in London in 1944 that
'America provoked Japan to such an extent that the Japanese
were forced to attack Pearl Harbour. It is a travesty on history
to say that America was forced into the war.'[1]

Yet in the last months of 1941 there were still widespread
doubts about any Japanese threat to the USA, most Americans
taking the view that Japan was still somewhat backward and
far too occupied with war against China to take on any other
nation. Lucas began to step up his inquiries into who was visiting Germany from Japan as well as into what the Japanese
were doing in Far Eastern areas outside their own jurisdiction.
Matsuoka, the Japanese Foreign Minister, was due to visit
Berlin and the indications were that he hoped to persuade the
Germans to put pressure on the French to accept a Japanese
move into Indo-China. This seemed unduly optimistic, but
what impressed Lucas was intelligence he obtained quite
independently from Hainan in the far south of China that
Japanese troops were being specially trained in jungle warfare
in great secrecy. This to some extent pointed not only to future
operations in Indo-China, but Malaya, Burma and the Dutch
East Indies.

Much more indicative of future plans, however, was the information from Heinrich Stahmer who had just returned from a mission to Japan. His news was that the Japanese were planning to organize advance parties of undercover agents into the areas they proposed eventually to invade. Many of these posed as Buddhist monks; in other cases an insignificant coolie on a rubber plantation might actually be a senior officer in the Japanese Army. One such was Colonel Yakematu who, on orders from Tokyo, went to Singapore and found himself a job as a coolie on a small rubber plantation on Singapore Island, using this opportunity to spy out the land and send in reports. Later he got a job as a longshoreman in Keppl Harbour, the key point for supplies at the Fort Canning headquarters, the fortress of Singapore. Next he moved to the naval base on Johore Strait as a construction worker before becoming foreman on a Japanese-owned rubber plantation near Tampin in the Malay state of Negri Sembilan where he set up a secret headquarters.

This information was passed on to some American Intelligence sources, but again it seems to have been dismissed as too improbable for words: 'if you can believe some Nippon colonel would work as a coolie, you must be out of your mind,' Lucas was told. Nevertheless Colonel Yakematu ultimately became head of a secret mission comprising some 180 Japanese army and navy officers.

Some were disguised as coolies, some worked as tugboat captains and fishermen; a few undertook labourer's work in the rubber plantations; others became truck drivers around the tin mines and on two airfields which the British were building. They recruited numerous agents from the local populations and, between them, charted the channels along the Straits of Malacca and studied beaches for landing operations. The boast in Tokyo — and there is still much to support it — was that the Japanese had a more detailed picture of conditions, defences and security in Singapore and Malaya than had the British themselves.

The problem in US intelligence at this time was a lack of skilled analysts to examine such information, and few indeed who could carry out independent checks on it. Furthermore, much of the intelligence from Lucas was actually discounted or mistrusted because it came from Germany. Consequently Lucas began to switch his attention to Japanese operations close to the USA either actually inside American territory or in adjacent countries such as Mexico and Latin America. He became particularly interested in what he saw as Japanese intrigues in the area of the Panama Canal Zone and beyond there in territories such as Costa Rica and Nicaragua. He was quick to sniff out a hint of possible espionage when he was told by an American deep sea fisherman, 'these goddam Japanese fishermen off the Californian coast are too crazy for words. Do you know they spend a hell of a lot of their time re-checking their charts and taking soundings?'

Lucas thought it was worth while making some more inquiries and he persuaded the American to take a closer look at the Japanese fishing vessels. The report came back that a number of yellow-painted drums were stowed on one ship. Careful inquiries revealed that the contents of the drums were being used for acid corrosion tests on a broken-down vessel. Lucas deduced that the true motive for these experiments could be to test the ability of the drums' contents to disable warships below the waterline.

He became certain that Japan had for some years been building up an intelligence service not only on the west coast of America but all along the Panama Canal. He noted that in Panama City there was a Barbers' Association of Japan which was under the control of a Japanese girl named Chiyo Morasawa who had come to Panama to run a clothes shop in the late 1920's. It seemed odd that such a girl should be directing a barbers' association. Then he learned that she briefed the barbers on what kind of information they should try to collect when US naval officers visited their premises. It did not take him long to find out that Chiyo Morasawa was married to a reserve officer in the Japanese Navy and that she frequently took photographs of military installations along the Canal.

Meantime the network, even though somewhat depleted inside Germany, was still functioning and "Olga" was managing to get quite a lot of information through to her Swiss base. She, too, stressed the probability of Japanese forays into South-East Asia, both in British and Dutch territories, while expressing the view that all the news coming out of Berchtesgaden suggested that as each week passed a German invasion of the United Kingdom was less likely. Other snippets of intelligence which came through to Lucas included German plans for moves in the Balkans and especially in the direction of Bulgaria and the Carpathians. As a result Wythe Williams was able to broadcast that: 'Another German army, of unknown strength, is assembling along the Danube in Rumania whence it could march through friendly Bulgarian territory, no doubt in exchange for Hitler's impending assignment of the southern Dobrudja to Bulgaria.'[2]

According to her own account of life at Berchtesgaden, "Olga" took some incredible risks on occasions when she was there. Once she heard that a detailed report had been prepared by Dr Heinrich Stahmer, the Far Eastern specialist, on his visit to Tokyo and that this was lying on Hitler's desk awaiting his attention. "Olga" went into Hitler's office and quickly read the notes while the room was empty. She took the precaution of taking some other papers into the room in case anyone came in and asked what she was doing.

Suddenly she was disturbed by noises on the veranda outside so she knocked on the French windows before stepping out into the presence of Hitler, Ribbentrop and Marshal Jodl. It was a nasty shock, but "Olga" coped with the situation by offering the papers to Hitler, saying she understood he wanted them urgently. Soon after this a tripartite pact between Germany, Italy and Japan was established.

It was partly as a result of this information that Lucas decided that it might be worth trying to obtain through some of his contacts copies of documents touching on relations with Japan from the German Embassy in Washington. The ubiquitous Klaus Mann, who seemed to be on close personal terms with various diplomatic couriers and one or two key people in the Washington Embassy, had apparently picked up some gossip to the effect that such papers existed and that they would shortly be sent on to Dr Stahmer in Tokyo.

'Where do these papers come from originally?' asked Lucas.

'They have been sent by Berlin.'

'Why, then, have they come to Washington if they are intended for Tokyo?'

'Because this is the safest means of sending them. The only

127

other way would be via Russia and if the papers got into Soviet hands, it might be disastrous.'

'But they might fall into Allied hands if they came across the Atlantic?'

'Ah, yes, that is so, but they are being sent through the medium of a Spanish diplomatic courier. That is how I found out all about it.'

Lucas, who was a stickler for detail in such matters, seemed satisfied by these explanations. He trusted Klaus, even though the latter's calculated air of mystery irritated him at times. His view was that Klaus cultivated this picture of himself as one deeply wrapped up in all kinds of mystery solely to impress. 'He is taking risks,' he told the doubting Wythe Williams, 'and, while anxious to help us, he also needs to help himself and to keep in with the Americans. I'm not worried about Klaus, but I do wonder whether at some time or other he is not going to be detected by the Nazis over here and probably exploited by them with bogus information.'

Lucas investigated further and discovered that Klaus's contact inside the Washington Embassy was a clerk named Heinrich Nostiz who was secretly critical of Nazi policies. What both Lucas and Williams most wanted was, of course, photographs of all the papers, but all he could produce were shorthand notes of the text. These, however, proved to be of the utmost importance, confirming fully all that "Olga" and others had reported.

Wythe Williams was not using such material for himself alone. He passed it all on to the United States authorities before receiving permission to publish some of it in a series of magazine articles. But he had some difficulty in getting it accepted. One editor refused to print, saying, 'such information is too frightening to give the American people.' However, a more courageous editor, Fulton Oursler, believed that the American people could take the information reasonably and without panic, and ran the articles in *Liberty Magazine* for several weeks.[3]

Not long afterwards Lucas heard from the network that some 140 Japanese officers, led by Lieutenant-General Tomoyuki Yamashita, had been received at Karin Hall by Goering. There was even a story, reported by Linda, that

Goering 'took this man Yamashita up in a Junkers 97 bomber and flew with him over London while the city was being pounded by the Luftwaffe. When they returned, Yamashita said that seeing the smoking ruins of the big city was one of the great thrills of his life.'[4]

There followed a broadcast by Williams to the effect that he had 'received a comprehensive report dealing with Japanese Foreign Minister Matsuoka's activities during his extended stay as a guest of the Soviets.... I am also in receipt of information that six Japanese divisions are on the island of Hainan, training in the complexities of jungle warfare. Since the terrain of Hainan is very similar to that of Malaya, the conclusion is obvious.'[5]

Not unnaturally, Wythe Williams tended to concentrate at this time on those items of intelligence which directly concerned the United States, and there was a great deal of Lucas's information on other matters, more directly concerning the United Kingdom, about which he made no reports. Most of these concerned the sensational flight to Britain by Rudolph Hess and the reactions to this inside Germany. First of all, Goebbels announced that Hess had flown to Britain and crashed to his death. There was a plan for three days of national mourning. Then came the news from the British that Hess had arrived in Britain and been taken prisoner. Goebbels was made to look a total fool. Everything was done to try to prevent this news being widely circulated in Germany, but to no effect: rumours of the wildest kind persisted.

But it was not so much in Germany as in the USSR that the Hess escapade created most serious concern. For the truth as revealed by Lucas's network, but not disclosed by Wythe Williams, was that Hess's private intelligence service had long since been infiltrated by Soviet Intelligence. They knew exactly what Hess had been planning, knew of his schemes for a peace deal with Britain and foresaw the problems that would be caused if he succeeded. What is more they were absolutely certain that Hess had full details of German plans for double-crossing their temporary Russian allies and declaring war on the USSR. Lucas was told that the man who had become Hess's chief of intelligence was none other than Captain Franz Felix Pfeiffer, generally known as Abeiltung Pfeiffer, and that he was a Soviet agent.

129

Herein lay the reason why Stalin always believed that Hess had given the British details of the proposed German attack on Russia and that Churchill had failed to keep him informed. Certainly Churchill behaved in a remarkably untypical manner in his personal handling of the Hess question. It may have been that he was temporarily unnerved by the feeling that there were still influential people in Britain ready to oust him and make peace with Germany, but one would have expected Churchill to react to this in a much more positive manner than he seems to have done. Not only did Churchill, who had an instinctive sense for the right kind of newspaper publicity, remain totally reticent, but he issued the remarkably strange order that on no account should Hess be photographed. As a result no pictures of Hess were taken during the whole time he was in prison in Britain. Duff Cooper, then Minister of Information, personally urged that photographs should be taken, arguing that if Hess ever managed to escape, the Government would have no proof that they had ever held him.

One reason, and one reason only, was then advanced personally by Lucas, and since then has been supported by a few. This was that the British had doubts whether the man claiming to be Hess really was Hess. Lucas had an open mind on the subject. According to one of his friends, Edwin G. Miller, this was the gist of Lucas's summary of the problem: 'Now we know that somehow the Russians were mixed up in all this, almost anything is possible. It is even possible that the Russians may have sent over a bogus Hess to Britain just to seek out information. If they had infiltrated the Hess Intelligence Service, they would know exactly how to exploit such a situation if only to learn what the British intended to do.'[6]

Did the British suspect some kind of plot surrounding the man claiming to be Rudolf Hess, or were they taken by surprise and somehow unable to come to terms with reality? Did the bogus Hess (if such he was) try to deceive the British by pretending to be mentally disturbed? 'Much learned medical attention has been devoted to Hess's mental state,' wrote Winston Churchill. 'Certainly he was a neurotic, a split soul seeking peace in the pursuit of power and position and in the worship of his leader.'[7]

The theory that a substitute for Hess was sent to Britain is to some extent supported by medical evidence. One senior surgeon at the Berlin Military Hospital is emphatic that the frail, senile Nazi who died in Spandau Prison was not Hess, while consultant surgeon Hugh Thomas, who treated the man called Hess for two years, is equally insistent that the man in question could not possibly be Hess. He bases his assertion on the fact that according to all medical records, which are confirmed by Frau Hess, Hess had a three-and-a-half inch scar on his chest, an injury from World War I. The man who died had no such scarring.

The question therefore arises, if the man who flew to Scotland was not Hess, what happened to Hess? Was he murdered, and, if so by whom — the Germans, the Russians or by some British Secret Service agent? Was he murdered before he could set out on his flight, or was he shot down while en route and a substitution made later? There is the interesting fact — surely something much more than a coincidence — that on the night Hess flew to Scotland, the Nazis launched the most extensive and severe bombing attack on Britain of the whole war.

There is no doubt that there was an earlier plan for Hess to travel to Spain and Portugal to make contacts with the British. "Olga" made independent reports on this proposal to her Swiss contacts. "Roger" states that Albrecht Haushofer, in response to a request by Hess, drew up a list of four names of Britons sympathetic to a peace proposal. 'As far as I can remember these names were the Duke of Hamilton, Sir Samuel Hoare (British Ambassador in Madrid), Lord Lothian (Ambassador in Washington) and Owen O'Malley, then British Ambassador to Hungary,' states "Roger". 'All this planning would be about September 1940 and Haushofer sent a letter to the Duke of Hamilton via Switzerland to propose a secret meeting in Lisbon. There were two mysterious trips to Switzerland by Haushofer in 1940 which included meetings with Carl Burckhardt, a Swiss diplomat and vice-president of the Red Cross. The contents of Haushofer's letters were passed to British Intelligence, and I would think they also reached the Russians. Certainly the Russians were well aware of Hess's schemes for a peace deal with Britain.'[8]

This largely bears out the late Sir Maurice Oldfield's belief that Hess's intelligence service had been infiltrated by the Russians. As a former head of MI6, Oldfield's statement on this is worth considering. It is true that he did not expand on this subject, but the mere hint was sufficient.

Much later "Olga", who was still responsible for feeding through some information of British interest, took the view that the British plan laid by a few secret service agents to lure Hess to Britain had been betrayed to the Russians and that it would, in consequence, end in failure. By failure, she did not mean simply that the peace plan would fail, but that the British would totally lose the initiative and make no propaganda out of it.

Pravda in 1943 declared that Britain had become 'an asylum and refuge for gangsters' and that, by being there, Hess would escape any punishment at the end of the war. Sir Archibald Clerk Kerr (later Lord Inverchapel), the British Ambassador in Moscow at the time and a notorious Soviet sympathiser, tried to reassure Stalin that after the war Hess would be charged like other Nazi leaders. However you look at it Britain seems to have created a quite ridiculous mystery out of the Hess Affair. Large numbers of original documents relating to the Hess case have been removed from files in the Public Record Office, and medical reports are also suppressed. Why?

There can be little doubt that one reason is the involvement of the Royal Family — not so much the Duke and Duchess of Windsor, who are usually blamed, but George VI and the Queen Mother herself. The truth is that some of the files concerning Hess are in the present Queen's private archives and that they may remain sealed to the public for ever. There was a lengthy period in which the King himself was not averse to considering German overtures. He had always been opposed to Churchill as Prime Minister and expressed his own preference for Lord Halifax.

Lucas was certain that the Hess plans for a peace deal with Britain were well worked out and stood a chance of success. He hoped that they would be defeated, but he remained in doubt until some weeks after Hess' arrival in Britain. 'It could have been touch and go,' he said, 'and the British may never know how near they were to being totally sold out to the Nazis.'

None of this material was used in Williams' broadcasts or in the columns of *Greenwich Time*. Both Williams and Lucas took the view that any hint of such deals could not only aid the Nazis, but also destroy any American belief in Britain's ability to survive. How right they were.

13

WORKING FOR G-2

For some time after the German invasion of Russia in 1941 both Lucas and Williams suffered from delays in communications from their network. Lucas felt sure there was a much tighter control on the courier service and that in some way this affected whatever means of communication his agents used. Then came bad news from Washington. The man inside the German Embassy in Washington, who had helped to provide details of the confidential records to be sent to Stahmer in Tokyo, was dead. He was alleged to have died inside the Embassy from "heat prostration", but Lucas feared that the Gestapo had eliminated him and that there had been an attempt by the Germans to suggest he had committed suicide. After that Lucas began to worry that a similar fate might overtake Klaus Mann; but Mann seemed to be a great survivor.

It was shortly after this that a letter from "Olga", written in the security of Switzerland, told of her own problems. She had received a secret message from Gottlieb, when she was visiting a favourite mountain resort in Germany, which read: 'You are no longer safe at your home or at the Berghof ... Go immediately to B----- and remain there until you hear from me ... They have been advised by me and will take care of you. Destroy this at once.'[1]

Not surprisingly, "Olga" was alarmed, for she knew that Gottlieb was not one to panic. She immediately burned the note and made her way across country alone to the small hostelry in the mountains which Gottlieb had indicated. There she remained hidden until arrangements were made for her to escape into Switzerland. This turned out to be a much slower process than "Olga" had imagined, involving a lengthy drive in a truck to a barn where she was told to hide in the hay-loft for the night. In the morning she felt somewhat reassured in looking out at a large stretch of water. This, she had told herself, must be the Bodensee, with Switzerland on the opposite bank.

But it was not easy to cross the water in safety; heavily armed German patrol boats frequently cruised around, at night piercing the darkness with their searchlights. It was more than a week before her rescuers decided it was safe to try to get her to the Swiss shore.

This was, of course, the kind of emergency for which Lucas had made financial provision in Switzerland, and "Olga" was safe, though Gottlieb was very much the man in the hot seat in view of what had happened first to Wolfgang and then to "Olga". He was forced to call a halt to any activities from his few close informants for the time being, as he could not be sure if he himself was under suspicion or being watched. He had already taken a big risk in organizing the escape of "Olga", and he was also worried that Linda might in some way be linked to "Olga".

Nonetheless, from inside Switzerland "Olga" herself revealed an astonishing talent for organizing intelligence out of Germany, quite independently of her friends at Karin Hall and Berchtesgaden. She obtained details of the Russian campaign after Hitler had ordered the invasion of the USSR territories. There were also warnings that Hitler was anxious for a diversion away from the Russian front. Ideally, it seemed as though he wanted to see an attack by the Japanese on Russia, but according to "Olga" this was out of the question. Japan had no interest in waging that kind of a war; what she wanted was swift and easy acquisitions in South-East Asia. Lucas himself continued to take the view that the United States would lose out in negotiations with Japan for any peaceful settlement of outstanding differences if only because of the pro-Soviet, anti-Japanese lobby inside the US administration. 'Ultimately,' he urged, 'Japan will declare war on the USA.' Not only was his advice ignored, but when Wythe Williams sought to put this view in a number of magazine articles he was bluntly told to hold back anything on Japan.

It was Linda, who eventually came through with what seemed to sum up the whole situation realistically. In a letter which arrived via South America she wrote: 'Oshima has asked Hitler point-blank whether Hitler will implement that part of the Tripartite Pact that calls for Germany to declare war against the United States if Japan does. The Japanese militarists take the viewpoint that any movement southward will constitute an outright gamble unless they succeed in taking the Philippines at the same time. They contend that to leave this American outpost on their flank would endanger their entire enterprise. Therefore they want to go to war against the United States at the same time that they open hostilities against the British Empire.'[2] It was the very kind of situation which Hitler had not envisaged when he first pressed Japan towards war against Britain. Belatedly it dawned on him that he was being drawn into a trap which meant he would have to go to war against the USA while he was heavily engaged in war with the USSR.

Not long after this America was forced to face the facts of life by the Japanese attack on Pearl Harbour.

From then on both Wythe Williams and Lucas were placed under the most drastic censorship and each knew that he owed it to the United States to provide full cooperation in the war effort. As Williams himself put it, 'information of any kind belonged first to our authorities in Washington, to be released as and when they deemed best, under the rules of wartime censorship.'

Not that Williams got much thanks for his patriotism even when he went out of his way to cooperate with the authorities. He had acquired many enemies in the course of editing *Greenwich Time* and making various broadcasts. There were still some who condemned him as either a stooge of the Nazis (grossly unwarranted) or as a mere publicity seeker. He cited the case of one bank manager who said of him 'this chap Williams seems to know so much about Hitler, he's probably in league with him.'

Once the USA was involved in World War II Williams offered his services on a non-profit making basis and they were accepted by an independent New York station: only rarely in this period was he able to present exclusive information, partly because of censorship, but equally as a result of the difficulties of retaining contact with the network in Germany. Even when he secured such information, with Lucas's cooperation, it was still presented to the US authorities first.

As to Lucas he lost no time whatsoever in offering his services to the United States, and, as usual, he had his own suggestions as how he could be of most value. His main idea was that he wanted to track down all the key Gestapo appointments not only in the USA, but in Central and Latin America as well, for he was convinced that by this time German plans included forming fifth columns in all countries in the Western hemisphere. He had arranged, long before the USA was at war with Germany, for a watch to be kept on the German Tourist Bureau on 57th Street in New York City. There he had discovered a key figure whose job it was to organize a gang of stevedores to collect intelligence on ships bound for Europe. Through this source Lucas slowly but surely compiled a list of Gestapo representatives in New York, Chicago, Boston, Cincinatti, St Louis and Philadelphia. With some of these people he was able to strike up an acquaintanceship and he gleaned something of what they were trying to build up. This was in effect a dossier on the various sixteen million Germans by birth or extraction living in the United States, both citizens and non-citizens, to be used to blackmail these people into assisting the German cause.

The whole campaign was conducted with Teutonic thoroughness, and it also probed into these people's links with Germany, via relatives and friends. Prior to the USA being involved in World War II the Gestapo had, of course, quietly followed up the findings of the dossier by visiting a number of such families in the USA. Sometimes the Gestapo were able to make their point by hinting at trouble or arrest of a relative at home in Germany. Rather more rarely they offered financial assistance in exchange for certain information. Tactics varied according to the situation, and for those in key posts the temptations were made greater.

'I don't think the Gestapo will have as much success inside the United States as they hope for,' said Lucas, 'but where they will gain ground is in Central and Latin America. Once the USA is brought into the war, the drive in those territories will be accentuated.'

For the rest of the war it was in this very area that Lucas

mainly operated. Having offered his services to the US Authorities, he became in 1942 an agent of G-2, the military intelligence branch of the Army. In a statement which he made while staying in Acapulco, Mexico, in March 1944, Lucas told an official US interrogator that 'two weeks after Pearl Harbour I went to Washington and offered my services free of charge to the War Department. I've gone on several missions for G-2 and they pay only my expenses. However, twice they gave me bonuses that ran into four figures, and I did not return either cheque.'[3]

He added that the War Department 'would not allow him to write or publish anything of a subversive nature he had received after Pearl Harbour.'[4]

Nevertheless he was still able to write some detailed articles based on information coming out of Germany. In December 1942, he reported how 'reports from inside Germany — and they arrive regularly despite Nazi vigilance — stress the point that Goebbels is launching a fresh campaign of deception against the American public. It is, in fact, a renewal of the campaign of a year ago when the propaganda genius deliberately planted stories in neutral capitals — Stockholm, Ankara, Berne, Madrid, Lisbon — forecasting an imminent German crack-up from within.'[5]

Lucas told how, immediately following Pearl Harbour, Goebbels submitted his idea to Hitler to 'capitalize on the American propensity for accepting unfavourable reports about the enemy. He planned to make us believe that the war could be won without any great effort. He wanted to keep us complacent.'

In this same article Lucas pointed out that recreation was one of the outstanding factors in maintaining morale in Germany. During the summer football, tennis and other matches were staged in every sizeable community, while in smaller circles cycling, bowling, hiking and swimming were encouraged. The Nazis had even injected the trick of recreational travel awards to war workers who distinguished themselves. After the fall of France excursionists were taken to Paris to shop. During the following winter the Italian Riviera and Naples became favourite goals. The gist of Lucas's warning was that there was absolutely no sign of the Germans cracking up on the home front and that in their offensive against South Russia they had imported some 800,000 German, Hungarian, Dutch and Danish farmers as supervisors of and workers on what formerly constituted the Soviet's collective farms. They were also transferring additional thousands from bombed cities in Western Germany. In short, victory could only be achieved by a tremendous effort against a formidable enemy. At the same time Lucas was well aware of the need for America to keep watch on the influence Germany was trying to exploit and extend in the southern American states. He was, of course, cognisant of the fierce opposition which the newly created OSS faced from the armed services, the State Department and the FBI as well as from some of the White House staff. General Donovan had access to the President and could explain to him the importance of clandestine operations, but he found few others would listen to him and many would oppose him. William Casey, later to be head of the CIA, who worked for the OSS in this period, stated later that 'you only had to be around the OSS a few days in the summer of 1943 to realize how embattled an organization it was ... It is no exaggeration to say that Donovan created the OSS against the fiercest kind of opposition from everybody.'[6]

Edgar G. Hoover, chief of the FBI, saw in Donovan someone who threatened his own domain, though this was totally without justification. This resulted in the FBI closely monitoring anybody who was recruited to the OSS or any other Intelligence service. Detailed reports from the FBI, and others, on Lucas round about this time reveal how closely he was being watched and assessed, yet often without any good reason. Hoover's almost manic-suspicious mind directed at his would-be allies resulted in the creation of his own Special Intelligence Service (SIS), a clandestine counter-espionage unit. In sifting through documents of this period which have been released for inspection it is sometimes difficult to tell when "SIS" refers to Hoover's unit or to the British Secret Service, not least when the name of the SIS informant is blacked out.

It may have been thought that someone inside the FBI thought that Lucas was being given too much latitude, or too much money, as queries on payments were always being raised. Perhaps the authorities were puzzled by some of what they regarded as Lucas's eccentricities. Titles and honours of foreign origin have never been fully approved in the USA and there was the fact that Lucas's visiting card described him as "Lieutenant-Colonel, K.G.", (which of course referred to his membership of the Order of the Knights of St George.)

Possibly what worried the authorities most was his steadfast refusal to say how he had obtained the German Military Code and who his informants were. The FBI reported that Lucas told them the "best scoop" he had been able to obtain through his sources of information was relative to the French–German armistice in 1940. 'The subject related that he had been able to intercept a message between Germany and the German military attaché in Madrid, and that because he had a copy of the German Military Code, he was able to decipher the message. The subject gained this information three days prior to the time that the armistice was announced to the general public.'[7]

Lucas went on to say that his friends in Germany were 'the Fifth Column in that country,' adding that refugees and other persons fleeing from Europe were unable to furnish much information of value. When it was suggested to him that the British were the only people who had intelligence agents in Germany, he replied: 'Oh, don't worry, we [the United States] have got them there, too.'

It was, of course, understandable to some extent that both Military Intelligence and the FBI should find almost unbelievable Lucas's achievements in building up his own network of agents right across Europe and even into Russia. Curiously, they seemed at this particular time to be much less interested in his Russian connections. Some of these officers may well have wondered whether he was not running some kind of a racket to con people into thinking he knew far more than he did. Yet they certainly seemed to make unnecessary work for themselves in conducting their inquiries, sometimes using three "watchers" at a time merely to find out which shops Lucas, his wife and daughter visited on their travels, or what he ordered in a hotel lounge, and, more than once, going through his suitcase and papers when he was out of his room.

One FBI report stated 'The surveillance of Lucas during this time was carried out in a manner calculated to render discovery impossible and at no time during the pertinent period was there any doubt in the minds of the surveilling agents that Lucas was completely ignorant of their activity. It is believed therefore that the entire surveillance of Lucas, for which the Office of the Legal Attaché in Guatemala might be responsible, was carried out so that there was never any danger of the subject becoming aware of the fact that he was under surveillance.'[8]

Nevertheless, one can be quite sure that so shrewd an operator as Lucas would soon become aware that he was being watched. On his return to Guatemala City on one occasion he was questioned by a Colonel Cruse concerning the identity or description of a person Lucas believed to have been surveilling him. This much was recorded in another FBI report which mentioned that 'Lucas stated he had been placed under surveillance while he was near the Salvadoran border and that the surveillance continued until he arrived at Guatemala.' He also advised that on 1 March 1944 he had been under surveillance from Guatemala City to Chimaltenango as well as during a trip to Quezaltenango. This mystery appears not to have been cleared up.

Lucas continued to stress that the number of German agents in the Western hemisphere was being stepped up all the time, and that there were three hundred such agents being trained in Madrid in a school known as *Hispanidad*, also known as the "House of the Americans". It was linked to the Spanish Falange and supported by German funds.

In another report Lucas told his G-2 colleagues that the provision of United States birth certificates had become a racket which was being exploited by the Germans. 'Nazi agents can buy them for fifteen or twenty dollars apiece from some official and come and go freely into the United States. Last year we caught three of them.'

At the same time he claimed that his inquiries had shown that there were 3,000 Nazi agents on the German payroll in Argentina, which he described as being 'the most heavily Nazi-infiltrated area in Latin America. A German can easily buy a passport there and travel to Central America. Somebody from Honduras travelling on a Honduras passport to Argentina sells it to a German agent who can easily change the photographs and other descriptive data to suit himself and then use it to travel to Central America. The person who sold the Honduras passport and to whom it was originally issued has only to apply to the Honduras Embassy in Buenos Aires in order to obtain a new one, telling the Honduras authorities that he has lost his original passport.'

Some time before this Lucas went to Havana in an effort to locate the meeting place of what he had been told was a gathering of the principal Gestapo agents in the Western hemisphere. He had heard that the original instructions for this meeting had been issued in Miami. Eventually he linked up with one of his German informants in the network, a character known as Manfred. He was astonished to find the man had managed to get away from Hitler's field headquarters, where he had been posted for a long time. He also learned that Manfred had applied to join the staff of Reinhardt Heydrich, Himmler's chief aide, when the former made a trip to Latin America, and that the application had been accepted. Manfred explained that the party had been given Spanish passports and had flown from Dakar to Brazil and then on to Havana where the secret Gestapo briefing meetings were held on a large plantation in the Pinar del Rio province to the south-west of Havana. His informant reckoned that there were seventy-eight key agents at the meetings. The main subject under discussion was what was called "the German Plan" for Latin America, and the USA. Latin America was to be divided into five separate Gestapo areas all of which would be directed by the leader of the groups in Buenos Aires. It was from this invaluable source that Lucas acquired the names of key Gestapo agents in such places as Brazil, Argentina, Chile, Colombia, Guatemala, Venezuela and the USA as well.

During the course of their association Lucas was occasionally blamed for something Wythe Williams was said to have done, or *vice versa*. After the war Williams made the comment that 'Bill and I were always getting each other out of scrapes, usually scrapes not of our making.'

One such was when some old friends of William's returned to New York from Europe and accused him of having broadcast for the Nazis in occupied France. They seemed astounded that he had dared return to the USA. 'But,' replied the equally astonished Williams, 'I have never been out of New York, and I certainly have made no such broadcasts.' Eventually he was able to convince them, and immediately tried to find out what had given them this impression. He learned that the Nazis had used his name for one of their propagandists broadcasting from various of their stations in occupied Europe after he had ceased his own radio talks in the USA, in order to suggest he had switched his allegiance to Hitler.

'This probably means that the Gestapo have rumbled us at last — at least they have rumbled you, if they haven't quite got round to me as yet,' was Lucas's comment.

Early in 1944 this enthusiastic hunter of Nazis reported to G-2 that he had had information to the effect that a secret German mission had arrived in the vicinity of Viedma on the coast of Argentina and that they had first visited Buenos Aires and then gone on to Santiago. Immediately G-2 followed this up and learned of another report that this mission had arrived in San Salvador from Bogota for one week, 'during which time they were contacted by leaders of the German underground organization in the five Central American countries.'

By this time Lucas had secured the names of key Nazis and Gestapo agents in Latin America and was particularly interested in the name of Eberhart Bedenklich who was in El Salvador awaiting a chance to get into the United States. Bedenklich was a native of Reutlinger in Wuerttemberg and, according to Lucas, had been using the name of Alphonso Fonseca, a citizen of the Republic of El Salvador. Lucas furnished the following description of Bedenklich to the US military attaché in Guatemala:

'Height: 5ft. 11ins. Build: stocky, but not stout. Eyes: brown. Hair: dark brown with grey fringe at the temples. Age: 41, but looks younger. Languages: German, Spanish, French and Russian fluently. English less fluently with an accent. Complexion: clean shaven. Occupation: formerly in Gestapo, now member of Foreign Section. Habits: smokes cigarettes exclusively.'

At the same time he supplied a few details of two other suspected senior Gestapo agents: Ferdinand Preisler, who had a Detroit birth certificate made out in the name of Jacob Hardy as well as Mexican papers in the name of Enrique Hernandez, and Heinrich Kuagelein, who had a Kansas City birth certificate in the name of Henry Maple, and Mexican papers in the name of Francisco Alfaro.

Once again Lucas was convinced he was being shadowed by somebody for he wrote to the military attaché from Quezalten-ango on 3 March 1944, saying: 'Unfortunately, since seeing you I have run into a few difficulties about which I shall tell you upon my return to Guatemala City. Thus far I have been able to cope with them. One is my being followed by someone across half of the Republic of Guatemala. As I do not know who my "watch-dog" is, I have found means to render this special attention ineffectual at such times when something is cooking, using a slang expression. I expect to have the gathering of information completed by the middle of next week, when I shall report to you again.'[9]

It would seem that somehow Lucas had managed to meet Bedenklich and win his confidence, as shortly afterwards Military Intelligence was advised that he had visited the city of Ayutla near the Mexican–Guatemala border and that he had in his possession shorthand notes, not yet transcribed, concerning excerpts from a report by Nazi agents in the United States to Germany. There was also a request from Lucas to Colonel Weckerling to make arrangements for General Harris in Mexico City to let him have six hundred dollars for expenses.

Eventually the report entitled the "German Plan" was delivered to the Military Attaché's Office by Lucas. It contained sixty-eight pages of double-spaced typewriting and covered many topics from the main objectives of Germany in Latin America, future conduct of the war, several paragraphs on their subversive efforts in Latin America, details on the effects of Allied bombings in the occupied countries, defences against the expected Allied invasion and aircraft production figures. The analysts appeared to be impressed by the report and its credibility and convinced that it must have been written by someone who had been inside Germany within the last month. They advised Military Intelligence that the report itself indicated that the information came from a person who was a Gestapo agent landed in South America from a submarine for the purpose of contacting other Gestapo agents in Latin America.

The FBI report on all this stated that 'Lucas advised Sources

E, F and G that the information in the report had been obtained from his contact, Bedenklich, on a *finca* near the town of El Progress, between Guatemala and El Salvador in the department of Jutiapa ... Lucas told them that he received this information from Bedenklich orally, while his daughter took the conversation down in shorthand notes. She later transcribed her notes and typed the report ... Lucas stated that he had given Bedenklich five hundred dollars in travellers' cheques, as well as a personal cheque made out in "cash" and drawn on the National City Bank of New York in the amount of two thousand dollars.'[10]

An attempt was made both before and after the alleged meeting with Bedenklich to track down the Gestapo man himself as well as to get confirmation of Lucas's story. Ultimately all the watchers reported that 'efforts to identify Eberhart Bedenklich resulted negatively,' this despite the fact that discreet inquiries had been made at every coffee *finca* in the Republic of Guatemala.

Somehow Lucas, doubtless with some assistance from his wife and daughter, managed to cover up his activities very effectively.

14

LUCAS WARNS OF THE
SOVIET THREAT

Lucas continued to stress that the bluff of "unconditional surrender" had in no way impressed Hitler and that the Nazi Party was sure of eventual victory, and he began to pay more attention to the long-term Russian threat. He stepped up his campaign to warn Americans that they would have to face the fact that the Soviet Union, far from being an ally, was soon to become their main enemy. This was regarded especially in official circles, as a piece of eccentric judgement. Once again Lucas had to face the fact that he was the bearer of unwanted tidings: too often in the world of Intelligence those who receive information dislike what they do not wish to believe.

Meanwhile his network continued to produce information on Germany which suggested that, despite such set-backs as the invasion of North Africa (which Lucas believed helped the USSR far more than the Western Allies), and despite the fact that Russia was beginning to stem the tide against the Nazi hordes, the High Command in Germany believed the key to victory lay to building an agricultural and industrial "Arsenal of the East". The dominant figure in all this was Colonel General Jodl, who had been busy working out a strategic plan of his own. The nine points of the Jodl plan, now in effect, are: 1. Hold the Fortress Europe and its approaches; 2. Convert Europe into a single military and economic unit [almost an early attempt at a Common Market!]; 3. Concentrate all sea warfare on the submarine weapon. Increase the construction of new U-boats to at least 250 a year, or five times the expected maximum losses. Since a U-boat sinks an average of 100,000 tons of shipping during its lifetime, this will compel the Allies to build 25,000,000 tons of shipping annually if they are to keep pace. 4. Conduct all future actions against Russia from a negative point of view — that is, destroy rather than absorb Russian means of existence so as to create an ever-increasing strain on Anglo-American replacement capacity.[1]

This all pointed towards a lengthening of the war and results less satisfactory to the Western Allies. One important point Lucas made was that the Germans were insistent upon maintaining and increasing 'the quietly functioning information channels from the United States. Do not antagonize the American people unnecessarily with industrial sabotage or token bombings. It is more profitable to sink the finished American products in the thousands of miles of vulnerable sea lanes than it is to hamper their production at home.'[2]

In a purely confidential memorandum Lucas argued that 'much time is being wasted and lost in the ill-planned invasion of Italy. All that is doing is to help the Russians indirectly. It has caused Germany to withdraw ninety-two divisions from the Russian front and send them to Italy. Until then the German Army had 220 divisions on the Russian front, so now the Russians are able to make some military gains and draw closer to realizing their plan of breaking out across Europe before the Allies get there. Both the United States and Britain have made the mistake of not requesting any specific aid from Stalin in return for this diversionary action.'

Reports were often delayed by the necessity for complicated and roundabout lines of communication, but still they came through. One said that 'at the end of last year [1943] there were 7,000,000 homeless in Germany as a result of the bombings. This destruction has united the German people in feeling they have everything to win and nothing to lose by remaining together under the Nazi regime ... Under the British theory of "area bombing", ninety per cent of the hits are scored on industrial targets ... Placing the damage to industrial targets at ten per cent was placing it very high indeed and above the general average.[3]

It remains a mystery how much Lucas learned directly from contacts he had made with Germans in Latin America, and how much he relied on his network inside Germany. His continued refusal to reveal the latter irritated the authorities, though reluctantly they accepted the need for such conditions.

He was able to warn that even early in 1944 Germany could spare a fleet of twenty cargo submarines to travel to Japan, bearing between 800 and 1,200 tons of freight at a time, including rubber, camphor and other materials vital to the war effort.

Following another report which he had submitted to the United States War Department Lucas said he intended to write an article on the subject for *Reader's Digest* magazine. Presumably he secured clearance for this: certainly he was insistent that 'the American people should know what's going on in this instance.' That article was entitled *Is a Soviet Europe in the Making?* and it was certainly one of the most keenly perceptive pieces of journalism at that time. Having stressed that the Western powers had taken up the Nazi challenge with the avowed purpose of erasing Nazism and 'making the world safe for our conception of the capitalistic system,' Lucas warned that the events of the past year had contributed towards destroying the illusion with which 'our country entered the war.' A world revolution was on the way, he warned, but instead of being a revolution of the Hitler brand, it was one led by Soviet Russia.

Of all pro-Soviet influences Lucas considered the most dangerous were 'the doctrinaires who advance the belief that a united Europe would be the medium of ending all inter-European wars. Originally they supported Hitler in his conception of the New Order as a means of merging the nations of the European continent into one political and economic system. Inasmuch as Hitler's policy of union by conquest has failed, they now reason that a European Soviet system might prove the proper answer.'

There is, however, no trace of any such article having been published in *Reader's Digest* under the name of either van Narvig or Lucas, though both of his other articles for that journal have been traced. One wonders if in this instance he was persuaded by the authorities not to submit an article which was critical of an ally in time of war. According to the FBI report this unpublished article went on to say that there was 'likewise every indication that Russia is preparing politically as well as militarily to assume the leadership in Soviet Europe. Largely owing to her sponsorship of the common term, Russia has a more efficient espionage system all over Europe than either England or the United States. Moscow is kept constantly informed on a change of political trends in every country under Nazi domination ... Exhibiting a far greater foresight than the Nazi leaders ever showed, the men of the Kremlin are clearly paving the way for the coming revolutionary changes in the political structures of Europe.'

Sometime between late 1943 and the summer of 1944 Lucas appeared to have obtained some new intelligence on Russian affairs which made him concentrate on such warnings. It is clear that someone had informed him about the extent to which the Roosevelt administration and the civil service beneath it had been dangerously infiltrated by agents of the Soviet Union. It was at this stage, too, that he appeared to have more foresight than many in suspecting that none other than that ace "Red-baiter" Joseph McCarthy could be a Soviet agent. Certainly history has shown that McCarthyism, whatever its original aims, proved to be a propaganda gain for Moscow. No doubt this view in turn created a great deal of trouble and suspicion for Lucas later on in the post-war period, the argument in those tense and often irrational days being 'if you are against Joe, you must be a commy dog.'

There are no files available in FBI records on this particular subject, but that is not surprising. There was an FBI investigation from 17 January 1952 until 19 October 1954 into inquiries about McCarthy, which included a probe into an article written in the *Las Vegas Sun* by Hank Greenspan entitled *Is McCarthy Really a Secret Communist?* An investigation has been developed earlier into this very question under the supervision of Major-General A.R. Bolling, Assistant-Chief of Staff, G-2. The only vital fact in the FBI released papers is that the transfer of the case to McCarthy's friend, FBI Director Edgar G. Hoover, was arranged through President Truman. The FBI files suggest that they limit their work to following up indications that McCarthy was a member of a homosexual ring which was already under investigation by G-2.

After a "New Deal" profile in the 1930's McCarthy was "born again" as a Conservative. He was a judge in Wisconsin and his 1946 Senate race here against Senator Robert M. La Follette, Jr. was his first major foray into politics. Yet the key to McCarthy's victory in this election was the bitter attacks of the Communist-dominated Milwaukee CIO against La Follette, whom they had earlier supported. The editor of *The Capital Times*, a Wisconsin newspaper, wrote in 1952, that 'McCarthy's self-proclaimed one-man crusade against communism is the creation of the Communist themselves,' and that he was associated with the 'Milwaukee-centred Trust agent Jacob Rubin, founder of the Odessa Soviet.'

The documentation shows close collaboration between McCarthy and Hoover in Hoover's burying of these allegations. The inspectors who investigated this case, C.C. Deloach and G.C. Gearty, stated in a memorandum of 23 January 1952 that 'Major-General Bolling was, of course, reminded that the Army's responsibility [G2 had also taken an interest in this case] stemmed from a specific request from the White House, and therefore we could not assume such responsibilities. He stated that he was very concerned over the delicacy of the situation, not only because of the delinquent status of the case, but additionally, because of the violations of protocol in that he was dealing directly with the White House and not through the Army Secretary of State Frank Pace.'

Lucas's theme was that behind all this was evidence that The Trust, the bogus organization set up by the Soviet Union in the early 1920's, was still being operated. "Trust Number Two", he called it, adding that "Trust Number Three" was probably already being planned to take its place the moment Trust Number Two came under the microscope. The object of the original Trust was to create a bogus anti-Bolshevik organization which would lure counter-revolutionaries and other enemies of the regime back to Russia where they would be promised underground support. On arrival they would be arrested and summarily dealt with by the authorities. Two skilled operators were chosen by Felix Dzerzhinsky, head of the Cheka, to carry out the planning. They were Yakushev and Opperput, who operated inside Russia under the cover of an organization calling itself the Moscow Municipal Credit Association.

"Trust Number Two" has not as yet been fully uncovered: indeed, despite an extensive CIA quest for information on it, and a lengthy analytical study, details are still lacking.

Realizing that US Intelligence was becoming more aware of the Soviet threat, the plan was for "Trust Number Two" to infiltrate the ranks of the more credulous and easily manipulated members of the anti-Red lobbies and to exploit these so that they and they alone would spearhead a campaign for rooting out Soviet agents. The object was to cripple a competent US counter-intelligence by the use of such bumbling clowns as McCarthy, and to put forward names of suspects who, under any close examination, could be shown to be totally innocent. Thus, in the end, the McCarthy campaign led to no worthwhile unmasking of Soviet agents, but by its fatuity and sometimes sheer imbecility in naming the wrong people, helped to create a public opinion which swung completely the other way. Thus McCarthyism proved to be a strategic gain for Moscow. The key figure in the manipulating of McCarthy seems to have been Jacob Rubin, the Wisconsin banker who was founder of the Odessa Soviet in the 1920's.

Who were Lucas's informants in this period? Were they German or Russian or both? To what extent had he built up informants among Americans? Obviously he continued to maintain his network and to keep in touch with them while working for G-2. But how did he manage to baffle the FBI when he met them? The truth is that all the lengthy and detailed reports made by the FBI while they watched Lucas and his family in the latter part of World War II there is nothing to suggest they ever tracked down his contacts, nor did they catch him out in any devious move. In evading such surveillance and keeping his contacts hidden, Lucas was not only supremely confident, but realistically efficient. It was always obvious that he had thoroughly studied the counter-espionage measures of other countries. In many ways the chief puzzle is why he did not enter some nation's Intelligence Service far earlier. The answer probably is that he mistrusted the majority of those who acted for the very countries in which he most believed.

There can be no question but that Lucas would have been an asset if used intelligently inside the OSS, possibly on missions into Europe. While his assistance in monitoring German intrigues and operations in Latin America was useful, he would have been far more valuable as an agent operating in

Europe. But even if the OSS had tried to recruit him, there is little doubt that this would have been opposed by some, not least by the FBI. William Casey, the late CIA chief who worked inside the OSS for Major General William Donovan in Washington, has stated: 'You only had to be around the OSS a few days in the summer of 1943 to realize how embattled an organization it was ... It is no exaggeration to say that Donovan created the OSS against the fiercest opposition from everybody — the Army, the Navy, State Departments, the FBI, Joint Chiefs of Staff, regular Army brass, the whole Pentagon bureaucracy, and, perhaps more devastatingly, the White House staff.'[4]

The OSS has never perhaps been given sufficient credit for its role in World War II. Despite the fact that Donovan and his new service acted all the time under constant restrictions, OSS actually worked hard to shorten the war by sending out accurate information which should have enabled coherent reports to have been made on German vulnerabilities, and by linking the American Armies with the underground Resistance forces. But far too often most of this information was discarded by the military. Again Casey recorded that 'at most Army headquarters OSS units were either liked or tolerated' and he noted that the First Army G-2, who rejected OSS help on his front, was the one who made the 'colossal intelligence failure' that permitted Hitler to stalemate the war by his secret assault on the Ardennes in December 1944.[5]

When war ended Lucas continued to produce articles for various papers, especially for the New York *Daily News* all under the name of William van Narvig, most of them warning about the threat posed to the Western world by Soviet Russia. At the same time, in the late 1940's and early 1950's, he had the idea of setting up a new organization to be called the Legion of Good Neighbours. In this he was backed not only by Wythe Williams, but many other people, including Colonel Edward Kirby, who had been Chief of SHAEF Broadcasting Services, serving on General Eisenhower's staff.

In a letter dated 8 September 1947 Lucas set out the ideas which had motivated him in proposing the Legion of Good Neighbours. He summarized these as follows: 'That since the differences between Western civilization, as represented by the

American way of life, and the Kremlin hierarchy are unbridgeable the Legion of Good Neighbours is intended to serve as the
moral equivalent of the atom bomb.' He went on to say that
the Soviet World and the Western World were engaged in a
cold war which, it was feared, could in due course develop into
a hot war. 'The United Nations thus far has shown much in the
way of futility and impotence ... one-half a glorified debating
society and one-half an arena for jockeying for world position
... Much of the futility displayed by the UN is traceable to the
fact that it operates on the level of governments exclusively
and that under the democratic system governments are
compelled to do a great deal of political jockeying because their
tenure of office is dependent upon political voting trends ...

'The Legion of Good Neighbours is a non-political, non-
profit, non-denominational, non-sectarian educational institute
of members who aim to promote world peace. The Legion is
formed to promote and develop the spirit of good neighbours
and to teach and foster the democratic way of life; to promote
citizenship and understanding among people at home and
abroad, to conduct forums, lectures, radio programmes and
other public functions towards the accomplishment of bringing
the citizens of the Western hemisphere into closer contact and
understanding, and to develop the spirit and create the incen-
tive towards the promotion of universal peace and goodwill
among the people and nations of the earth; to establish
committees and other media for the avoidance of future wars
and to eliminate class hatred, bloodshed and needless destruction of culture and civilization in an atomic age which renders
mankind helpless, except through a unity of understanding and
goodwill.[6]

There was nothing particularly original in this project. It
would seem to have been among the most harmless of organizations and Lucas's own statement, while lucid, was certainly
lacking his usual forthright punches and occasional touches of
unorthodox humour. For once, it looked as though he had bent
over backwards to remain discreet and simple in all he said.

Nevertheless his project led to an FBI report which covered
some nineteen pages of detailed research into the Legion of
Good Neighbours. What was the FBI looking for? Had the
"Reds under the bed" bug already bamboozled the FBI as later

it was to upset the whole nation under Senator McCarthy's relentless and obsessive campaign? Or had McCarthy put the boot in for Lucas?

FBI files show quite clearly that detailed inquiries were made not only into the Legion but into its backers, including Wythe Williams and others as well as Lucas himself. One file shows that 'this investigation is predicated upon Bureau letter dated 4 November 1947 and a letter from Vincent Quinn, Assistant Attorney General, to the Director, dated 24 October 1947. These letters request that an investigation be conducted relative to the Legion of Good Neighbours and more specifically that the activities and contacts of Wythe Williams and William Otto Lucas, also known as William van Narvig, be developed.'[7]

The FBI inquiry was indicated in its title as follows: 'William Otto Lucas, aka William van Narvig, Colonel William van Narvig; Wythe Williams; Legion of Good Neighbours: character of case — mail fraud.' One of the FBI reports cited a letter to ... [name blacked out] dated 8 September 1947 in which Lucas set forth 'several of the principal considerations which motivated the project of the Legion of Good Neighbours. These considerations are summarized as follows:

'That the differences between Western civilization as represented by the American way of life and the Kremlin hierarchy are unbridgeable. Van Narvig sets forth that over a period of years he has enjoyed the acquaintanceship, even friendship, of A.A. Zhdanov, currently looked upon as Stalin's heir presumptive. He states that he has discussed world affairs with Zhdanov on many occasions and that while he respects him as an individual and a family man, the deep gulf which exists between his conception of a world order and the American conception on the same subject is something else again.'[8]

Wythe Williams was cited as having stated that the Legion of Good Neighbours was intended to serve 'as the moral equivalent of the atom bomb,' adding that the UN was a 'great and noble institution but it unfortunately suffered from one great handicap in that it operated on the level of governments only. The LGN, while functioning on a parallel with the UN, would do so on the level of the people themselves.'[9]

The certificate of incorporation of the League was filed at

New York on 13 November 1947, and it gave as its purpose exactly the same wording as Lucas himself had supplied independently. The certificate also stated that the number of directors should not be less than five, nor more than twenty. There were various suggestions as to how the League could be developed, with chapters being set up all over the USA and a proposal to reach mass audiences by means of the radio on a programme to be called *The Good Neighbour Show* which would be presented weekly on a nation-wide hook-up. There was also to be a publication called *The Good Neighbour*, and it announced that the LGN hoped to enlist General Dwight D. Eisenhower to head its special Board of Strategy.

The people cited as being behind the project were, apart from Lucas, Wythe Williams; Colonel Edward Kirby (listed as having been Chief, SHAEF Broadcasting Services, serving on Eisenhower's staff); Paul Robert Thoma; Katherine Leeds, of Riverside Drive, New York City; David Williams of the same address; Frank D. Chaiken, of Brooklyn, New York; and William B. Campbell, of New York City.

The FBI probe into the LGN referred to a letter from "William van Narvig" in which he stated that 'we have discussed our ideas at the White House and with Secretary of State George C. Marshall. They were looked upon with favour and received the promise of friendly cooperation whenever needed. Which is all we want from official Washington, since under the envisaged organization set-up we cannot possibly contemplate any financial governmental support.'

Once again the FBI built up a dossier on Lucas. They noted that the Hall of Records, Brooklyn, revealed a deed, recorded 27 May 1946 under the name of William Otto Lucas for the private dwelling located at 247 93rd Street, Brooklyn, and that a mortgage on this property was recorded by the Bay Ridge Savings Bank, Brooklyn. Notably, the FBI report stated that 'Lucas has the local respect and goodwill of neighbours in the immediate community. No derogatory legal information was set forth.'

The other individuals who backed Lucas were also investigated in some detail, again without finding anything in the least derogatory. Paul Robert Thoma, one of the men behind the idea, was described as 'a well-known Hollywood producer–

director for Warner-Brothers Universal Pictures,' but more disturbing is the fact that the names of various "confidential informants" are blacked out. In the FBI files is a letter from Lucas (though his name is signed as "William Van Narvig") to someone whose name is blacked out, writing on the subject of the Good Neighbours. He is appealing for support. The letter is interesting in that it exemplifies Lucas's passion for baseball. 'Only yesterday,' he writes, 'I witnessed an incredible event at the fourth World Series game at Ebbets Field, Brooklyn. A completely outplayed team, with odds 54 to 1 against it, came up in the last split-second to win a game in the most fantastic finish ever recorded. Even a fiction writer with the wildest imagination would never dare put a thing like this in his book. And yet, there it was — an indisputable fact. But it only happened because there was in the man a great tenacity of effort, a persistent refusal to give up.'

Membership fees for the LGN were 'regular membership ten dollars a year; sustaining membership fee [whatever that might be] 100 dollars a year; honorary membership 500 dollars a year.'

Possibly Lucas sought to make a new interest and career for himself in launching the LGN, but the whole FBI probe into its affairs seemed to be a waste of time. Nothing whatsoever was found in evidence against the LGN or Lucas himself. But it was now obvious that he had many enemies, and that some of them had prompted the FBI probe into the League of Neighbours. Maybe this alone stifled its progress. It is even possible that somehow the Russians had come on his trail and were attempting to cause trouble for him with the Americans. For by now his articles under the van Narvig pen-name were totally hostile to the USSR.

One wonders whether the death of his friend, Zhdanov, contributed to this. Zhdanov had gradually worked his way up the hierarchy of the Soviet Union from when he became head of the Communist Party organization in Nizhni Novgorod in 1924. From 1939 onwards he had largely shaped the ideological aspects of Stalinism and their interpretation into policies. During the siege of Leningrad in World War II he played an important role in the defence of that city. He was also generally believed to have been the chief instigator of the "winter war" against Finland. For his services in defence of Leningrad he was given the rank of Colonel-General. On 21 August 1941 he aroused Leningrad's workers to patriotic fervour with a speech which declared that the city was in grave danger and that they had 'a revolutionary role to defend it.' As a result 400,000 men, women and children marched out to dig trenches and fortifications.

It was Zhdanov who built the highway stretching 400 miles right over the ice of frozen Lake Ladoga to supply Leningrad from the north, a superb feat of engineering. In December 1942 it was possible to make a modest increase in Leningrad's rations, but Zhdanov refused to do this: food reserves must be maintained for the Army, he ruled, even if a few thousand civilians should die as a result.

Thousands did die, but Zhdanov apparently managed to get through to Lucas a message to the effect that children below the age of five had all been evacuated before the siege started, while those remaining and those born during the siege were specially fed and housed. This statement was confirmed after the war by Brigadier George Hill, the SOE British representative in Russia. It was probably because of Zhdanov's efficient, if ruthless methods of defending Leningrad in this period that after the war his birthplace, the Ukranian city of Mariupol, was re-named after him. Two districts in Moscow and Leningrad were also named Zhdanov.

Though ideologically poles apart, Zhdanov, like Lucas, seems to have had a respect for and sentimental feelings about some things in Russia's Czarist past. In yet another of the messages he smuggled through to the USA was his account of how he had given orders at the start of the siege of Leningrad (formerly St Petersburg) to protect the little wooden house on an island built by Peter the Great while the city he founded was under construction. This wooden house was covered in concrete and protected so thoroughly that its destruction even by a direct hit was almost impossible. It remained intact throughout the war.

After the war Zhdanov was president of the Allied Control Commission in Finland, a somewhat haphazard and ill-conceived development from the viewpoint of the Western Allies, but from the viewpoint of the USSR he forged relations between the USSR and Finland on a new basis. In this respect he showed considerable skill, bearing in mind that the two nations had been at war until relatively recently. In 1947 he also played an important part in helping to create the Cominform as a successor to the Comintern, that somewhat over-exploited organization for advancing the cause of international communism. In a speech he made in October 1947, he stressed the fact that two blocs divided the world and insisted that the Western bloc was planning war on the Soviet bloc. Almost half of this speech referred to what Zhdanov called 'the American plan for the subjugation of Europe.' The following year he sent a message to a Cominform conference in Calcutta, saying that Burma, French Indo-China, the Dutch East Indies and Malay were 'ripe for the armed struggle against imperialism.'

Probably it was Lavrenti Beria, head of the NKVD, who set out to block any further promotion for Zhdanov. Beria became alarmed at a proposal to give Zhdanov complete control of nuclear espionage and thereupon too steps to check his powers. It is certain that Beria would have known through his NKVD officers all about Lucas's friendship with Zhdanov and his visits to Leningrad and Moscow. It is even possible he might have been concerned about Zhdanov passing information to Lucas. Not that there was ever any suggestion that Zhdanov was betraying Soviet interests in anything he communicated to his friend. It should be remembered that he and Lucas had much in common in the sphere of engineering and technology. At some time or other they had many years earlier not only studied engineering together, but been linked in engineering projects. It was because Zhdanov had helped to organize the huge automobile plants and various other factories that he had been awarded the Order of Lenin.

In February 1947 it was announced that Zhdanov had retired from the presidency of one of the two Houses of the Supreme Soviet at his own request. There was no explanation for this. Then in September 1948 Moscow radio announced his death and that his body would be brought to Moscow to lie in state in the House of Unions until the funeral at the Kremlin. All Soviet newspapers appeared on the day of the announcement with half-inch black borders.

For whatever reasons (none of which he disclosed officially

or in print) Lucas was convinced Zhdanov had been murdered. In an article he wrote in 1952 he simply stated that his friend 'at the time of his murder in 1948 — a death falsely ascribed to natural causes — he was ... heir apparent to Stalin.'[10]

What information had Lucas received to cause him to make this assertion? Was it a wild guess, or had he been given some inside information from Zhdanov's family or friends, or even from his own network? It was unlike Lucas to make guesses and present them as facts. Had he ever adopted this technique Wythe Williams would never have supported him, for Wythe was a stickler for facts and evidence to back them up. There is one other possibility, a remote one but nonetheless worth considering, that Zhdanov had realized that Beria was moving in against him and that he had considered defecting. Had he done so, his knowledge of plans for espionage on nuclear matters would have been of immense value to the USA.

There was a curious sequel to Lucas's allegations a year later when the Stockholm newspaper *Aftonbladet* stated that Zhdanov, 'one of the Soviet leaders mentioned in Moscow charges of "medical murder" had died of incurable cancer, according to a Swedish doctor, Professor Berven who had treated him. The newspaper added: 'The case was hopeless and Professor Berven is reported to have been much surprised at being called to a patient whom no doctor in the world could save ... Before Professor Bervan left Moscow the Russian authorities requested — according to our informant — a certificate testifying that Zhdanov's disease was incurable and that no Russian doctor had committed any mistake in his treatment.'

At the same time the *Stockholms-Tidningen* said that the fact that the doctors Vasilenko and Feodorov who signed Zhdanov's death certificate were not among the nine doctors accused of "medical murder" seemed 'to prove the incongruity of the terrible conspiracy charges.' A third Stockholm newspaper, *Dagens Nyheter*, commented: 'For some time past there have been signs that the chief of the Secret Police, Lavrenti Beria — perhaps the mightiest man in the Soviet Union after Stalin and Malenkov — has lost influence or been moved down the ladder of the hierarchy. This has not been established, but when the trial of the doctors begins we shall see the real people the Russian Government wants to get at and learn whose lives are in danger.'

It was Stalin himself, paranoically suspicious in his old age, who presided over a purge of Kremlin doctors suspected of being foreign agents, and the probe was only halted by the Soviet leader's death. This much was revealed in a report in *Moscow News* as late as February 1988 when it was stated that Efim Smirnov, a member of the Academy of Medical Sciences, said he visited Stalin at his Black Sea dacha before the middle of January 1953 and 'found him consumed with suspicion about the medical care given Party official Andrei Zhdanov and Bulgarian Communist leader, Georgy M. Dimitrov.' 'It's strange,' Stalin remarked to Smirnov, 'one doctor treated them and both of them died.'

On 13 January 1953 the official TASS news agency announced the arrest of a 'group of terrorist doctors' said to be responsible for the deaths of Zhdanov and another official, A.S. Shcherbakov. These doctors were then accused of being recruited by a US intelligence front that TASS described as an 'international Jewish bourgeois-nationalistic organization.' Many of the doctors arrested were Jewish, and this heralded a resurgence of officially sanctioned anti-Semitism.

All this may have been a cover-up propaganda exercise to detract attention away from actual crimes committed by orders of the Soviet Establishment, but here again this is mere surmise. What is significant is that Lucas raised the question of Zhdanov being murdered long before any hints of this crept into the world's press. His information must have come from inside Russia.

From 1952 onwards Lucas became as positive in his opposition to the USSR as he had been to Nazi Germany. Under the Truman regime nobody in authority seemed ever to listen to him. He concentrated on writing for a living, using the van Narvig pen-name. One article of his described how approval of a plan for a massive Communist offensive to overrun South-East Asia was one of Josef Stalin's last official acts. The details of this scheme, he claimed, had just been disclosed in reports smuggled out from behind the Iron Curtain. The plan was that while the French Army in Indo-China was expecting a Vietminh attack in force on its positions at Hanoi, the rebels would instead push across Laos to the Mekong River without encountering much opposition. At the Mekong they would be joined by the Thai People's Army of General Pridhi Panomyong and, in due course, by the Burmese Red troops of General Thakin Tan Tun. The Soviet plan, expounded by Marshal Sokolovsky, was that the combined armed forces of these three "liberating" generals, given Chinese military supplies in sufficient measure, should secure total success.[11]

Shortly afterwards an attempt was made to put this plan into action. Three spearheads quickly pushed to the heart of Laos, one group swinging south to Paksane and the others avoiding meeting the French and Laotian defenders at the royal capital of Luang Prabang and the Plaines des Jarres. Then, suddenly, the Reds to the north of the capital began retreating and those in the south stopped advancing. Various reasons were put forward: failure of supplies, the approach of the rainy season, the Reds' sudden realization that the invasion threatened to interfere with the truce talks at Panmunjom.

In July 1953 Lucas gave his own explanation of this so-called failure. 'Because the Red Chinese leaders became convinced they were being used by Soviet Russia to pull the Kremlin's chestnuts out of the fire in Korea, the Peking government sought an armistice,' he wrote.[12]

'Reports smuggled from behind the Chinese lines indicate that Chinese Red dictator Mao Tse-tung has decided that Communist China will henceforth go her own way, even to the point of secretly combatting Russia for influence in Indonesia and South-East Asia ... relations between Russia and Red China became so strained that Mao Tse-tung made it plain to Moscow some months ago that he had decided to make a face-saving truce with the United Nations in Korea, whether Malenkov liked it or not.'

Lucas pointed out that the Kremlin's flow of help to China had diminished to a mere trickle and that Mao had begun to realize he had been lured into a very poor and one-sided bargain with the USSR. This particular article was one of the very last, if not the last, which Lucas wrote under the van Narvig name. Once again it was stressed by the newspaper itself that 'the information contained in this article comes from well-informed secret underground sources in many parts of the

Red world.' An earlier article carried a preamble that in his frequent trips to Russia the author had 'formed contacts which serve him today from behind the Iron Curtain.'

Shortly after this much of what Lucas had prophecied and described either came true, or was confirmed from other sources. This should have been the very moment when his reputation as a writer with inside knowledge on world affairs was at its highest, yet it seems to have been the time when in this respect he faded into oblivion. Was there a subtle campaign against him? There is the extraordinary affair of the FBI inquiry into the League of Good Neighbours. At the head of that report under the sub-heading "Character of Case" are the words "mail fraud". There is no explanation as to why that reason for investigation was given in the first place and nor, in the whole lengthy report, is there any evidence of or even allegation of mail fraud. Despite all inquiries, nothing against Lucas or the League was ever revealed in any of the papers. Yet the League itself seemed to be doomed to failure from the moment the FBI began to investigate it.

15

THE GROUP OF THREE

It was towards the end of 1954 that Lucas seemed to fade completely out of the picture. Sometime before this he appeared to have moved permanently to Miami. Yet even when there he still took out his telephone number under the name of van Narvig. In a 1978 Miami telephone directory he was listed as William van Narvig, 8201 SW 41st Terrace, Miami. By 1980 his name was out of the telephone directory and there was no indication as to what had happened to him.

A search of the Dade County Department of Vital Statistics revealed no trace of either name from 1978 onwards. Checks with such sources as the Library of Congress, and the Overseas Press Club, whose documents have been given to the Journalism School at Columbia University, have also drawn a blank. Appeals by letters in various American newspapers and in the FILS, the journal of the National Intelligence Study Center in Washington, have produced no further information, not even from a member of his family.

This all recalls the mysteries of what happened to so many of what one might term "our better spies". Their stories nearly all end in mystery so that nobody can ever be sure just when they died, or if in fact they might still be living. Sidney Reilly is a classic case of this. But it remains very surprising that, in America of all places, such a man as Lucas could be allowed to vanish so completely, bearing in mind his services both journalistically and in the national interest.

Yet however much the mystery of the latter part of Lucas's life may remain unresolved, there is evidence that the campaign he urged was carried on, if only by a few. "Roger" is convinced that it did: 'Certainly "Olga" continued to function

163

as an informant, mainly to the Americans, but also to Lucas himself. For how long I cannot say, but I am certain that "Olga" was one of the people who passed through information from Lucas's various Moscow and Leningrad contacts, as well as from remaining contacts in Germany. I was myself slowly edging out of this sleazy world of Intelligence at that time, having realized that the USSR had ceased to be an ally of those of us who, while anxious to see the Soviets succeed, deplored their ruthless attitude to any concept of life other than their own.

'I understood that "Olga" was one of what she called "A Group of Three".'[1]

Who were the Three, other than "Olga"? "Roger" thought that Lucas was not a member of the Group, but that he was simply kept informed by it. 'My feeling was that the Group of Three had a dual purpose, the first and most practical being to safeguard themselves against all eventualities and the second being to use what intelligence they gathered to uphold a Western civilization view of life while keeping a close watch on Soviet manoeuvres, and, equally, to make sure there was no attempt to resurrect Nazism in Germany, Austria or elsewhere.' What is not clear is to what extent they passed on information to other Intelligence Services. My own hunch is that they tried them all out in turn — American somewhat cautiously, British, even more cautiously, the new German Services, the Italian and the French. Possibly even the Swiss, though of this I cannot be sure.'

"Roger" would not even hazard a guess as to the identity of the other two members of the "Group of Three". How, therefore, did he know for certain that there was such a group? 'First of all I should stress that this was something which was talked about in those circles which had been mixed up in intelligence-gathering during the war,' he replied. 'People who had acted as agents were asking one another what they now planned to do when the war ended. I remember hearing from two or three sources, that, linked to "Olga", was what was repeatedly called a "Group of Three". It had been formed to maintain a permanent independent intelligence unit which would aim at safeguarding its members and ensuring that their work was carried on.'

Another who had heard of the "Group of Three' was Alexander Foote, who had operated radio contacts between the "Dora" network (run by Sandor Rado) and Moscow. It is his story after the war which becomes vitally important in tracing the missing links in the Lucas saga. Rado had pleaded with Moscow for close cooperation with the British, but nobody in the Kremlin would listen to him during the war. Indeed, Foote stated that on one occasion 'Rado suggested that the best thing for the network and himself would be for him to take refuge in the British Legation [in Berne].' The Centre in Moscow declined to allow Rado to do this. In the end he slipped across the border to France, but Foote was arrested in November 1943 by the Swiss. He was treated fairly leniently and eventually released on bail on 8 September 1944, making his way to the Soviet Embassy in Paris. Here both he and Rado were questioned separately by Soviet Intelligence. On 6 January 1945 the two agents were sent off to Moscow on the first Soviet plane to leave France after the liberation. Both were travelling with Russian repatriation certificates.

Rado was worried because the discovery of the radio transmitting stations by the Swiss was indirectly his fault: he had ignored a warning by Foote that there were probably two traitors in the network. When the plane stopped en route at Cairo, Rado took fright, believing that he was heading straight to his execution. He decided to seek sanctuary with the British and walked out of his hotel, leaving his coat and luggage behind to avoid suspicion, but carrying documents which identified him as a Soviet citizen. Meanwhile he cabled a friend in Paris who was in a position to corroborate his story to the British. This she did and it would, of course, have been very much in the interests of the British Intelligence to have had the benefit of Rado's knowledge, for he could have told them not only about the Soviet set-up in Switzerland but to some extent that inside Britain, too.

But it was not to be. On instructions from the British, the Cairo police arrested Rado and had him extradited to Russia. 'Even if they were not interested in Rado's fate,' wrote Arthur Koestler, 'they ought to have prevented his illegal extradition to the Russians, as Rado was not a Soviet citizen and his repatriation papers were a fake. I don't know for how many weeks Alex [Sandor Rado] stayed in Cairo, and whom Lene [his friend] approached in Paris. I only know that Lene's frantic efforts to save him were in vain ... it is only one detail in the vaster nightmare of the Western democracies bungling their relations with Russia during the later stages of the war and the early post-war years ... Alex Rado, the gentle, lovable, scholarly master-spy was one of the victims of the Occident's guilty ignorance and homicidal illusions.'[2]

Despite this, Rado survived, though only after spending ten years in a Siberian labour camp. Foote was more fortunate. This brave amateur spy did not try to escape in Cairo. He continued to Moscow where he was interrogated intensely over a long period. The NKVD were unsure as to whether or not he had been a British agent all the time. He quickly realized that if he did not adapt to the Party line, he would never be allowed to leave the USSR and might find himself in a labour camp, and he seems to have adapted successfully. He lived in a block of flats at 29, 2nd Izvosnya Ulitza, occupied mainly by families of Red generals. Here he managed to acquire a number of lady friends, though in effect he was a semi-prisoner.

The Russians waited until all *Abwehr* and *Nachrichtendienst* archives which they had captured in Berlin at the end of the war had been sifted. Foote was cleared when they discovered the treachery of their two agents in Switzerland and their pretence to the *Abwehr* that they could bribe the Englishman to come over to the German side. Then, early in 1947, Foote was informed that he was to be entrusted with the re-building of a *Razvedka* network in the USA from a headquarters which he was to establish in Mexico: 'My arrest by the Swiss as a Soviet agent had made it impossible for me to work again whilst living under my own name and I left for East Berlin to establish a German background for a new identity.'[3]

When Foote returned to Britain after defecting from Russia in Berlin he gave the Intelligence authorities every assistance. For a while he settled down as a minor civil servant in the quiet bureaucratic backwater of the Ministry of Agriculture and Fisheries. In effect Alexander Foote had made the most effective penetration of the Soviet Secret Service Britain had yet achieved and at the same time the Russians would never be able to deny that he rendered them service of incalculable value. Of all the people who played the Soviet game perhaps Foote is the most to be admired in that at the back of his mind he felt he was always serving the best interests of his country, while at the same time he had a great sense of loyalty to his paymasters. In contrast to the despicable Philby he was what one could almost describe as a wayward paragon. He could have defected back to the British when he reached Paris, but he decided that his duty lay in giving his Soviet masters all the information he had acquired since his arrest. When he left the Soviet Secret Service he still had a fair amount of money in a Swiss bank. Then, in his absence and almost three years after he left Switzerland, he was tried before a military tribunal in Lausanne and sentenced to two and a half years' imprisonment plus a fine of 8,000 Swiss francs and confiscation of all cash and property in Switzerland (all his worldly goods, in fact) and to fifteen years' expulsion from the country for contravening Swiss neutrality.

Now, the Swiss had previously treated Foote leniently, at least to the extent of showing some kindness to him during his imprisonment, and had eventually released him on bail. Was some subtle pressure brought on them by the British? Did someone in Intelligence or Counter-Espionage circles plant on the Swiss false evidence against Foote? "Roger" is quite sure that this is what happened. 'Smears against Foote were being passed around in diplomatic circles shortly after he returned to Britain. Somebody in London was damning Foote.' The answer to this may lie in Foote's own statement that 'having a fair amount of money in a Swiss bank, I intended to write stories of my adventures at leisure in England. But I was kept incommunicado by MI5 for almost three months, first in Hanover and then in London, before being set at liberty. One month after my release, and while I was in London, came my trial in Switzerland.' After that, of course, when Foote decided to write his book, *Handbook for Spies*, he was forced to accept that his story must be written and published under MI5 supervision. Foote's version of events would have been embarrassing to the pro-Soviets in both MI5 and MI6.

Foote felt he was totally misused by the British Intelligence authorities after he returned to London. He thought that the British should have let him go ahead as a double-agent by establishing himself as a Soviet controller in Mexico. 'I was told that all Resident Directors of Soviet espionage had been withdrawn from activity in the territory of Russia's co-belligerents in June 1941 and that numerous dormant sources of information in the USA were to be reactivated.' This was only half the truth, but it was nevertheless an indication of the Soviet's new plans for spying on the USA from adjacent territories. Foote went on to say that his reception by his British interrogators in Germany was distinctly hostile, even to the extent of his being informed that 'I should not take it for granted that I should be allowed to return to England ... I would point out that if at the time of my defection I had been persuaded to continue my work with the Soviets, with the secret cognizance of British Intelligence, very possibly the latter would now be in the possession of facts and information about *Razvedka* activities which at present they do not have.'[4]

I only had one fairly brief interview with Foote in the early 1950's and this mainly concerned my interest in 'van Narvig' whose real name I did not then know. Foote had heard of him under the code-names of "Werther" and "Walter" and said he understood he was a naturalized American, but he could tell me little else about him except that — I quote his own words — 'he left behind him a kind of international mini-network of three people, two of whom were based in Switzerland after the war. "Olga" was one member, another was a Soviet defector who had been in Zhdanov's entourage in Leningrad and the third was Wilfred Noyce, the British mountaineer. Noyce was a frequent visitor to Switzerland and he maintained the British connection with the network.'

Foote died on 1 August 1956, in University College Hospital, London. He had swung over from being pro-Soviet to supporting any Conservative MP who would listen to his case. Alas, there were too few of these around at that time. He maintained to the end of his days that there was treachery in high places in Britain and that he was constantly frustrated in bringing this to the attention of the authorities. His estate amounted to a mere £1,756 and he left no will.

I wish I could have questioned Foote in greater detail, but at that time I was mainly concerned in trying to establish the identity of "van Narvig". But I am quite sure that, while Foote knew exactly to whom I was referring, he had no knowledge of his real name. At that time I was less aware of the infiltration of the British Establishment by Soviet agents and therefore paid less heed than I should have done to Foote's insistence that (this was after the Burgess — Maclean defection) 'in view of recent events in this country it appears to me to be in the interest of security that the reason for the apparent failure of our Intelligence to draw any benefits from my defection, should now be studied by the Committee of Privy Councillors set up by the Prime Minister.'[5]

The name of Wilfred Noyce is interesting and it certainly points in the direction of Lucas because Noyce was a great friend of Professor Pigou and they went mountaineering together. "Roger" recalled that a certain amount of material from Cambridge received by his network concerned airfields, dispositions of squadrons and addresses of top secret stations. 'I remember we got information about aircraft being used for clandestine operations in Europe. Pigou himself through his ex-pupil, Wilfred Noyce, secured intelligence on squadrons formed on Newmarket racecourse in 1941 [he told me as much after the war when we all three met], and a year later we had news of the setting-up of a very hush-hush, camouflaged air base at Tempsford, not far from Bedford.'

Noyce was initially influenced by Pigou's pacifism and joined the Friends' Ambulance Unit at Edgbaston, later working with them in the East London hospitals. However, as the war developed he changed his mind and served first as a private in the Welsh Guards and then as a subaltern in the 10th King's Royal Rifle Corps. One of Noyce's Army comrades at this time, Mr Richard Holmes of Jesmond, confirms how when they were stationed not far from Cambridge Noyce took him to meet Pigou in his rooms in King's: 'The beer, brewed on the premises, was the strongest I have ever tasted ... it certainly loosened our tongues ... There was no doubt about the rapport which existed between Pigou and Noyce and ..., especially on the Soviet Union which they constantly praised and drank toasts to ... They clearly worshipped each other.'[6]

Another person present at that meeting confirms what "Roger" has stated — that Noyce certainly discussed with Pigou 'plans for setting up secret and camouflaged airfields in

169

the area around Cambridgeshire and Bedfordshire with the aim of putting supplies and agents into occupied Europe to help the Resistance movements. I was not paying a lot of attention at the time and they were talking fairly quietly. I don't think anyone else heard what they said.'

Afterwards Noyce was a captain in the Intelligence Corps in India. He even managed to do some climbing in the Himalayas during the war and became chief instructor at the RAF Aircrew Mountain Centre in Kashmir. He had two more terms at Cambridge after the war and then became a schoolmaster, first at Malvern and later at Charterhouse. In 1953 it was Noyce who, with Sherpa Annullu, opened the way to the South Coll in the successful ascent of Everest by Sir John Hunt's party. When Pigou died in Addenbrooke's Hospital in Cambridge in March 1959, after being taken ill at Zermatt the previous autumn, he left a proportion of his money to Noyce, including all copyright of his books and a share of the profits.

On 30 July 1962 it was announced from Moscow that Wilfred Noyce, together with another British climber, Robin Smith, had fallen to their deaths after a successful ascent of Mount Garmo in the Pamir Mountains on the borders of Russia and China. Noyce had already indicated that the expedition which he had led at the age of forty-one to Trivor in the Karakoram was his last, but when the Russians agreed to an Anglo-Soviet project, he felt such an opportunity 'of helping to breach the Iron Curtain was an imperative call ... with this in mind I accepted the invitation.'

It may seem somewhat odd that Noyce should let himself be mixed up in an organization, modest as it was, such as "The Group of Three". But he was in many ways a mixed up character, a restless, ever-questing romantic, permanently analyzing his own emotions. There is no evidence that he was ever involved in supplying intelligence to any foreign services in the way that Pigou had been. On the other hand he was deeply interested in international affairs, retained an affection for the Soviet Union, despite Stalinism, and at the same time hoped to make bridges between East and West. One cannot help wondering what "The Group of Three" developed into, whether they kept on plying Lucas with information, or eventually played a lone game on their own and possibly even sought to support a policy which Lucas regarded as unworkable in the current state of international affairs — achieving a friendly relationship between the Western democracies and the Eastern bloc. Certainly Noyce was of this frame of mind, constantly seeking ways in which he could personally involve himself in such a project. It should be remembered that "Olga", too, had helped Soviet agents with information as well as Lucas. The third member of "The Group of Three" remains a puzzle. I am certain that Alexander Foote knew his name, just as I am sure that he had himself kept up some kind of contact with Lucas even after he left Russia, if only on account of one remark he made to me. Referring to the Soviet plan for him to be sent to Mexico to organize espionage inside the USA, he commented: 'Just think of it, I should have been in a territory where I could always be visited by a pal — your van Narvig himself who is a frequent visitor to Mexico. What a merry game I might have played and all in favour of the cause of real Western freedom.'

16

IN CONCLUSION

Despite all efforts to trace what happened to William Otto Lucas after 1954, the latter part of his life remains an enigma. Nevertheless, even if at the age of sixty-one he faded out of the Intelligence game as a professional or a free lance (and who could blame him if he did?), and devoted his life entirely to his family for the rest of his days, he remains one of the most remarkable analysts of intelligence in modern times. Not even a writer of spy fiction has dared to think up the story of a spy who could claim to have had equally good contacts inside two such totalitarian nations as Nazi Germany and Soviet Russia. To have been able to visit each of these nations in a time of world war would have been unthinkable to most people, whether spy or spy-master.

False trails abounded in my attempt to solve the mystery of Lucas's life from 1954 onwards. Why, for example, did he maintain his pseudonym for his telephone number? It was the one name by which both enemies and friends knew him. One line of inquiry produced the information from Mr Alan J. Beevers, who had known him when he lived in Brooklyn, that 'Lucas was exasperated by the way in which he had been treated. He felt he was always being shadowed by somebody or other, if not by the Feds, than some other official agent. He had been one of the biggest critics of Averill Harriman, who was Director of Foreign Aid under the Mutual Security Act at that time. He thought Harriman was playing along with the Russkies too much, linking up with people like Armand Hammer. That didn't do him any good with the US administration which backed Harriman. He even believed that

Harriman was an ally of what he called "Trust Number Two".[1]

This may have been true, and quite possibly he was under some pressures from certain circles in Washington. However, yet another story was that even in Florida he was shadowed by KGB agents and that he had to move about from time to time to avoid their attentions. In the light of his article, published in 1952-3, this is quite feasible. Finally, I had a report that his death had been recorded in 1975 during a visit to the Bahamas. But there was no positive confirmation of this.

I must admit that for some years during my search for the Super-Spy of the twentieth century I feared that he was only a mythical figure, that just possibly he had been invented by Wythe Williams, even though I was supposed to have been introduced to him in New York in 1942. I am delighted that documentary proof has been supplied to show he was indeed real, not least the personal account of his life from the *New York Times*, who informed me 'the autobiographical statement by Lucas which was obviously written by him and dated in his own handwriting in April 1936 ... would not have been accepted unless authenticated.'

Whether any lessons can be drawn from this narrative is a subject upon which all Intelligence chiefs might usefully ponder at leisure. There is still a tendency for such chiefs (and even more frequently their subordinates) to dismiss offers of disinterested inside information from members of the public with contempt, if not suspicion. It was years before anybody listened to Lucas and long after he had proved his value he was still under suspicion. Nor was he the only able amateur spy to suffer a similar fate. Bernard Newman, the author and civil servant, used to spend his holidays cycling around Europe. He was once in danger of being sacked because the British Foreign Office objected to a book of his entitled *Danger Spots of Europe*. With the approach of World War II Newman kept an eye open on his travels for any sign of new developments in German or Italian arms production (he was banned from Italy by Mussolini). He was the first man to make a report on the V2 rocket when, in 1938, he came across some installations built on reinforced concrete and surrounded by barbed wire on the Baltic coast at Peenemunde. (A friendly hotel-keeper told him the

place was used for experiments for a new type of rocket.)
However, both the British Secret Service and the War Office
foolishly ignored his report.

The vital lesson surely is 'ignore such people at your peril'—
even if they may at first seem to be cranks or myths.

CHAPTER NOTES

CHAPTER 1

1. *The Dusk of Empire: The Decline of Europe & the Rise of the USA*, Wythe Williams, Chas. Scribner's Sons, New York, 1937.
2. *Ibid.*
3. Preface by Lowell Thomas to *Secret Sources: The Story Behind Some Famous Scoops*, Wythe Williams & William van Narvig, Ziff-Davis Co., New York, 1943.
4. A *History of the British Secret Service*, Richard Deacon, Frederick Muller, London, 1969.
5. Apart from the *Nedelya* article of June 1966, further information was given in the Russian émigré paper, *Russkaya Misl*, 8 June 1972, in an article by Revolt I. Pimenov, a Soviet dissident. He claimed that Reilly did not die in that 'carefully staged frontier incident', but that he was a Soviet spy all the time.
6. *Reilly: The First Man*, Robin Bruce Lockhart, Penguin Books, 1987.
7. Letter to the author from Mr Bernard L. Yudain, of Greenwich, Connecticut, 28 February 1983.
8. Dept. of State (Washington) confidential memo. No. 91, of 12 March 1940, released 7 July 1982.
9. *Secret Sources, Williams & van Narvig.*

CHAPTER 2

1. *Witness*, Whittaker Chambers, André Deutsch, London, 1953.
2. Letter to the author from Jukka Rislakki, 9 March 1981.
3. *Ibid.*
4. Cable from Sir William Stephenson, 18 January 1982.
5. Letter to the author from Mr Bernard L. Yudain, 10 December 1981.
6. Letter to the author from Wythe Williams, 3 June 1953.
7. Public Record Office, Kew: FO 800/317 H/xv/312.
8. Letter to the author from Wythe Williams, 17 June 1953.

9. Statement from "Roger", 24 January 1982.

10. *Secret Sources*, Williams & van Narvig.

11. Statement marked "Record of Experience" written and signed by Lucas, and certified by the *New York Times*, dated April 1936.

12. *Ibid*.

CHAPTER 3

1. *Ibid*.

2. Letter from Mr John C. Hodgson, 17 March 1982.

3. *Secret Sources*.

4. Reference to Dept. of State memo. no 91, of 12 March 1940: the initials of "H.V.J." on the paper suggests that Liddell contacted Johnson at the US Embassy in London.

5. Cited by William van Narvig (Lucas) in an article entitled "Pipeline to the Kremlin", *New York Daily News*, 13 October 1952.

6. *Secret Sources*.

7. FBI Papers on William van Narvig, 6 April 1944, File No. 8-3-52, 65 — 1 6107 — 1971.

8. Letter from Mr Bernard L. Yudain, 5 October 1987.

CHAPTER 4

1. Not all sources of information on Lucas were blacked out in the declassified records. Source E was stated to be Captain Archer B. Hannah, assistant military attaché in Guatemala City, and Source F was Colonel Fred Taylor Cruse, military attaché for Central America.

2. FBI Files No. 8-3-52, Mexico, D.F., 6 April 1944: title of report: "William D. Lucas, William van Narvig."

3. *Ibid*.

4. FBI Files dated 2-9-44, 2-10-44 and 2-17-44.

5. FBI Files 65 — 16107 — 1971.

CHAPTER 5

1. Letter from Mr Kyril Zinovieff to the author, 24 August 1987.

2. Letter from Mme. Nina Berberova to the author, 26 August 1987.

3. *Ibid*.

4. *Ves' Petersburg*, years 1909-1912, which gives a complete list of residents and is published in the Cyrillic alphabet. See British Library: (shelfmark p.p. 2458 yc).

5. Lucas's statement marked "Record of Experience".

6. The Pigou diary of 1905 was based on a 9-cell key in which the letters of the alphabet are disposed in groups of 3. The entries cited are for 21 and 24 August [Deacon Papers].

7. *Pilgrim to the Left: Memoirs of a Modern Revolutionist*, S.G. Hobson, Edward Arnold, London, 1938.

8. Letter dated 14 February 1918, from the *Delnicke Listy* files, Ohio.

9. *The Revolutionary Movement in Britain: 1900-21*, Professor Walter Kendall, Weidenfeld & Nicolson, London, 1969.

CHAPTER 6

1. Lucas's statement marked "Record of Experience".

2. *Ibid.*

3. Article entitled *Pipeline to the Kremlin*, by William van Narvig, New York *Daily News*, 14 October 1952.

4. Letter to the author from Reino Hatsonen, 7 December 1985. The book in which Mr Hatsonen saw the picture he claimed to have recognized as that of Lucas was *Errittain Salainen — Vakoilu Suomessa* [*Top Secret Spying in Finland*], by Jukka Rislakki, Love Kirjat, Helsinki, 1982.

5. *Ibid.*

6. Lucas's statement marked "Record of Experience".

7. *Ibid.*

8. *Ibid.*

9. Article entitled *Pipeline to the Kremlin*, van Narvig, 14 October 1952.

10. *Ibid.*

11. *Ibid.*

12. *Ibid.*

CHAPTER 7

1. *I Was Stalin's Agent*, W.G. Krivitsky, Hamish Hamilton, London, 1939.

2. Personal statement to the author, 17 June 1981.

3. *Secret Sources.*

4. Hobby-Lobby Radio Programme, WOR Mutual Broadcasting System, August 1939.

5. Cited by "Roger".

6. Article entitled *Pipeline to the Kremlin*, by William van Narvig, New York *Daily News*, 14 October 1952.

7. There is some evidence that this story was deliberately leaked to a number of European sources. It was a story which circulated in French Intelligence circles and Miss Elka Schrijver, of Amsterdam, confirms that her brother, then an interior decorator who had been employed by the Duchess of Windsor when she was Mrs Simpson, received a phone call (allegedly from

someone in the British Foreign Office) asking him to go to Paris to contact the Duke of Windsor and tell him to go to Germany where he would be proclaimed King of Hanover!

8. *Pipeline to the Kremlin* article, New York *Daily News*, 14 October 1952.

9. *Ibid.*

10. *Secret Sources.*

11. *Reilly: The First Man*, Robin Bruce Lockhart, Penguin Books, 1987.

CHAPTER 8

1. *Secret Sources.*

2. *Ibid.*

3. *New York Times Book Review*, 8 August 1943: review of *Secret Sources* by S.T. Williamson.

4. Letter from Mr Bernard Yudain, 23 May 1988.

5. PRO: Cabinet 24/260, pp. 6-10.

6. Documents relating to the eve of World War II, Dirksen Papers, vol. ii, 1938-39.

CHAPTER 9

1. *Handbook for Spies*, Alexander Foote, Museum Press, London, 1949.

2. *Ibid.*

3. From a memorandum of Foote's not previously published.

4. *Handbook for Spies.*

5. *Ibid.*

6. *Gazette de Lausanne*, 17 February 1949.

7. *Memoirs of a Conservative: J.C.C. Davidson's Memoirs & Papers*, 1910-37, ed. Robert Rhodes James, Weidenfeld & Nicolson, London, 1969.

8. *Honours for Sale*, Gerald Macmillan, Richards Press, London, 1954.

9. Personal statement by "Roger".

10. *Alpine Journal*, no. 64,

11. *Handbook for Spies.*

12. *Manchester Guardian*, 6 November 1953.

13. This theory is advanced in *La Guerre a été gagnée en Suisse*, Pierre Accoce and Pierre Quet. See also *La Chasse aux Espions en Suisse*, Col. R. Jaquillard, Lausanne, 1947.

CHAPTER 10

1. *History of the British Secret Service*, Richard Deacon, Frederick Muller, London, 1969.
2. *The Godfrey Papers: The Naval Memoirs of Admiral J.H. Godfrey*, vol. viii, Churchill College Archives, Cambridge University.
3. *The Schellenberg Memoirs*, by Walter Schellenberg, André Deutsch, London, 1956.
4. *The Mask of Merlin: A Critical Study of David Lloyd George*, by Donald McCormick, Macdonald, London, 1963.
5. *Secret Sources.*
6. *Liberty Magazine*, 19 July 1941.
7. See also *Urania's Children: the Strange World of the Astrologers*, by Ellic Howe, William Kimber, London, 1967.
8. *Volkischer Beobachter*, 14 May 1941.
9. Letter from Nicholas Campion to the author, 9 July 1984.
10. *Le Monde*, Paris, 26 August 1987.
11. Letter from M. Jean d'Ormesson to the author, 23 November 1987.

CHAPTER 11

1. W.O.R. Mutual Broadcasting System: 28 February 1940.
2. Statement to the author by "Roger".
3. *The Code-Breakers*, by David Kahn, Weidenfeld & Nicolson, London, 1966.
4. W.O.R. broadcast: 13 May 1940.
5. W.O.R. broadcast: 5 August 1940.

CHAPTER 12

1. Associated Press dispatch from London to New York, 21 June 1944.
2. W.O.R. broadcast: 8 October 1940.
3. *Secret Sources.*
4. *Ibid.*
5. W.O.R. broadcast: 17 April 1941.
6. Statement by Edwin G. Miller to the author.
7. *The Second World War*, by Winston Churchill, London, 1950, vol iii.
8. Statement to the author by "Roger".

CHAPTER 13

1. There is confirmation in Switzerland, not only from "Roger", but from other PAKBO sources that this story of "Olga", more usually known as "Clara" in Wythe Williams' accounts of her activities, is absolutely true.

2. *Secret Sources.*

3. FBI file on William O. Lucas, 65-16107-200.

4. *Ibid.*

5. *Reader's Digest,* article entitled "Goebbels Will Fool Us If We Don't Watch Out", December 1942.

6. *The Secret War Against Hitler,* William Casey, Regnery Gateway, Washington, 1988.

7. FBI file 65-16107-200 (Lucas).

8. *Ibid.*

9. *Ibid.*

10. *Ibid.*

CHAPTER 14

1. *Reader's Digest,* article entitled "How Hitler Plans to Win", April 1943.

2. *Ibid.*

3. This report from Lucas was cited in FBI files 65-16107-185.

4. *The Secret War Against Hitler,* Casey.

5. *Ibid.*

6. FBI Files, 12 February 1947, 36-3581-8.

7. *Ibid.*

8. *Ibid.*

9. *Ibid.*

10. Article entitled *Pipeline to the Kremlin,* by William van Narvig, New York *Daily News,* 13 October 1952.

11. Article entitled *Invasion of Laos Follows Strategy Mapped by Stalin,* by William van Narvig, New York *Daily News,* 11 May 1953.

12. Article entitled "Truce Tips Peiping's Plans to Grab South-East Asia", by William van Narvig, New York *Daily News,* 30 July 1953.

CHAPTER 15

1. Statement by "Roger", 14 December 1977.

2. *The Invisible Writing,* 2nd volume of *Arrow in the Blue, an Autobiography,* Collins with Hamish Hamilton, London, 1954.

3. Personal statement by Alexander Foote, 3 June 1954.

4. *Ibid.*

5. *Ibid.*

6. Personal communication to the author of Mr R.J.C. Holmes, of Jesmond, Newcastle-upon-Tyne, 1977.

CHAPTER 16

1. Averill Harriman (deceased) was President Roosevelt's Special Representative in Britain in 1941 and later became President and Chairman of the President's Special Mission to the USSR with the rank of Ambassador. He was a Special Assistant to President Truman from 1950-51, after which he became Chairman of the NATO Commission on Defence Plans and much later an "Ambassador-at-large". When Armand Hammer created the Allied American Corporation (Almerico) to open an asbestos concession in the Urals, he worked with the assistance of Isaac Hoorgin, a director of the German-Russian Transportation Company, which was a joint enterprise of the Soviet government and the Harriman interests in New York.

INDEX

INDEX